# How and Why We Teach Shakespeare

In *How and Why We Teach Shakespeare*, 19 distinguished college teachers and directors draw from their personal experiences and share their methods and the reasons why they teach Shakespeare. The collection is divided into four sections: studying the text as a script for performance; exploring Shakespeare by performing; implementing specific techniques for getting into the plays; and working in different classrooms and settings.

The contributors offer a rich variety of topics, including:

- working with cues in Shakespeare, such as line and mid-line endings that lead to questions of interpretation
- seeing Shakespeare's stage directions and the Elizabethan playhouse itself as contributing to a play's meaning
- using the "gamified" learning model or cue-cards to get into the text
- thinking of the classroom as a rehearsal
- playing the Friar to a student's Juliet in a production of *Romeo and Juliet*
- teaching Shakespeare to inner-city students or in a country torn by political and social upheavals.

For fellow instructors on Shakespeare, the contributors address their own philosophies of teaching, the relation between scholarship and performance, and why in this age the study of Shakespeare is so important.

**Sidney Homan** is Professor of English at the University of Florida and Visiting Professor at Jilin University in the People's Republic of China. The recipient of many teaching awards, he was recently chosen as the Teacher/Scholar of the Year at the University of Florida. He is also a member of the Academy of Distinguished Teaching Scholars. Author of 16 books on Shakespeare and the modern playwrights, he is also an actor and director in professional and university theatres.

# How and Why We Teach Shakespeare

## College Teachers and Directors Share How They Explore the Playwright's Works with Their Students

*Edited by Sidney Homan*

Routledge
Taylor & Francis Group

NEW YORK AND LONDON

First published 2019
by Routledge
52 Vanderbilt Avenue, New York, NY 10017

and by Routledge
2 Park Square, Milton Park, Abingdon, Oxon, OX14 4RN

*Routledge is an imprint of the Taylor & Francis Group, an informa business*

*Library of Congress Cataloging-in-Publication Data*
Names: Homan, Sidney, 1938– editor.
Title: How and why we teach Shakespeare : college teachers
and directors share how they explore the playwright's works
with their students / edited by Sidney Homan.
Description: New York, NY : Routledge, 2019. |
Includes bibliographical references.
Identifiers: LCCN 2019005194 |
ISBN 9780367190798 (hardback : alk. paper) |
ISBN 9780367245672 (paperback : alk. paper) |
ISBN 9780429283192 (ebook)
Subjects: LCSH: Shakespeare, William, 1564–1616–Study and teaching.
Classification: LCC PR2987 .H57 2019 | DDC 822.3/3–dc23
LC record available at https://lccn.loc.gov/2019005194

ISBN: 978-0-367-19079-8 (hbk)
ISBN: 978-0-367-24567-2 (pbk)
ISBN: 978-0-429-28319-2 (ebk)

Typeset in New Century Schoolbook
by Newgen Publishing UK

MIX
Paper from
responsible sources
FSC™ C013985
www.fsc.org

Printed in the United Kingdom
by Henry Ling Limited

# Contents

# Introduction: How and Why

*Sidney Homan*

My mentor in graduate school, a wonderful scholar and teacher, once confessed that he thought the only door closed more tightly than the bedroom was the classroom. He meant that faculty never just dropped into a colleague's class, never intruded on his or her space during that special time of interaction between teacher and students. "We listen to each other at conferences, review each other's books, discuss this and that author while walking about on campus. But we never go into someone else's classroom, never 'spy' on them—there's the word—while they're teaching." Now, having been in this profession for almost 60 years, I'm not sure this is completely true anymore. I myself have team-taught, and on occasion have been asked to visit the class of a young colleague up for tenure. Still, my experience has been that, at least in English departments, we speak to each other about what we teach, but not so much about what we do and how we do it.

## In Pursuit of "How"

There are several fine books I would point out that deal with teaching: for example, G. B. Shands's *Teaching Shakespeare: Passing It On*, which offers "anecdotes and practical advice" from various scholars who talk about their teaching in the areas of "Mentoring," "Text," "Text and Performance," and "Contexts (Institutional, Cultural, Historical)."[1] Google "Teaching Shakespeare" and your hits will range from the Folger Shakespeare Library's Teaching Shakespeare Institute, TES or Teaching Shakespeare (the collaboration among the Royal Shakespeare Company, the British Museum, the British Film Institute, Into Film, and the Victoria and Albert Museum), to "How to Teach Shakespeare So Your Students Won't Hate It" and "3 Rules to Break When Teaching Shakespeare."[2]

I thought of the excellent teachers I knew and wondered what would happen if I asked them to write in an informal style about how they teach and what their classrooms are like. I knew that what they did as teachers would be inseparable from what they had said in print or, in several cases, their work as directors and actors. Predictably, each writer had a unique style, both in prose and approach, but whatever differences in style or strategy, common to all the essays was the insistence that the play be recognized as something ultimately meant for performance. If their discussion with the students used the play as a mirror for everything from modern-day racial tensions to #MeToo, from the lives of the students to current politics, still that mirror was a theatrical, not a literary, one.

## And the Question of "Why"

I asked the contributors "how" they taught Shakespeare. I did not have to ask them "why," for in their response to "how" was their own deep commitment to the study of Shakespeare and to its place at the heart of a liberal education.

But these days this question of "why" takes on a larger, perplexing, and often grave meaning in the light of current changes in, challenges to, and crises in higher education. And while this collection focuses on colleagues sharing with us their strategies for teaching Shakespeare, I feel it incumbent on me to take a few moments to put that "why" into the larger context of pressures on English departments, the humanities in general, and the function of universities in our society.

Enrollment in English department courses, and by extension Shakespeare, is declining. One writer reports that his department has seen a drop in majors from 850 in the spring of 2011 to about 500 today.[3] Another study found that of 45 English departments at PhD-granting institutions, only 5 had a Shakespeare requirement.[4] Overall, those majoring in the humanities have dropped from a total of 30 percent of all college majors to less than 16 percent during the last generation. Conversely, business has become the major of more than one in five American undergraduates.[5]

The reasons offered for this situation are many, from cultural or political to economic. Universities, it is argued, are increasingly becoming businesses, corporations, substituting financial success for the pursuit of knowledge. Knowledge is now seen less as a public good than as a commodity to be capitalized on in profit-oriented activities.[6] Conservatives attack the study of literature as a playground for the "elite." Education, some insist, needs to be more practical. One writer predicts that only in a few private universities will the humanities survive; "elsewhere, they will be little more than a relic of the past."[7]

But good teachers, teachers who explore Shakespeare with their students with conviction and passion, with the authority born of their scholarship or their own work in the theatre, cannot help but strengthen the argument for retaining the classic notion of what is at the heart of a college education. More bluntly, good teachers attract good students.[8]

Again, I did not ask my contributors to address directly the question of why they teach Shakespeare. I didn't have to, for inevitably, by definition, by their very nature as teacher–scholars, they do so in the essays that follow. Their sense of obligation to their students, their concern for their students, informs every line they write.

Universally, they approach the study of Shakespeare without insisting on right answers or a single interpretation. Studying the playwright is "an exhilarating reminder that there aren't correct answers, and that the open-ended nature of informed academic enquiry rather than the furnishing of approved wisdom is the proper business of education" (Russell Jackson). For one contributor who is also a professional actor, "Only by working theatrically with the text will you find the answer that best suits you. In this, I hope I am educating rather than teaching" (Nick Hutchison). Another found that his students' "divergent interpretations were simply the product of the different answers they found, based on the different questions they posed" (Cary Mazer). One writer says that "the sense of Shakespeare's significance that my students bring to class is often immensely conflicted, even contradictory, and can play out in unpredictable ways" (Patrick Hart).

A common aim is to shake up old assumptions, to question what has been received, to find something new—a process for which the teacher is a facilitator. One helps students find "avenues for the text to become surprising and dynamic, even subversive" (Andrew Hartley). In reminding us that the neatly printed whole text was not "the medium in which Shakespeare worked," one teacher's goal is "to estrange them from [one] medium" so he can "help students understand the ways that dramatic writing both transcends and is bound by the media through which we access it" (Paul Menzer). Students "have an increased desire to learn by exploring ideas freely and a decreased desire to live unplugged" (Liam Semler); another complements his remarks with the observation that "'Business as usual' just does not seem appropriate in a world that has changed so quickly and drastically" (Frederick Kiefer). How, a colleague asks, can she help her students embrace "potential insecurity" as a way of asking questions and thereby learning more (Miranda Fay Thomas)?

I asked the contributors to speak from personal experience, to address the reader in their own person, and this led to connections between the play's illusory world and the world outside the classroom. One writes of trying to help the student "rediscover the character as not merely a poetic dreamer with a frail grasp on reality, but as a character who engages directly with essentially real—indeed visually concrete—features of his world" (Joseph Candido). That the play has its own reality, even as it mirrors life outside the playhouse, was graphically illustrated by one student who worked onstage as a fellow actor with her teacher: "the most important thing an actor can know onstage is what she needs from her scene partner. I imagine that [my teacher who played the Friar] and I were generous scene partners to one another because we needed the same thing, arguably the same thing our characters needed: an ally" (Jerry Harp and Erica Terpening). Another essay describes how, in working with a scene partner in an "open rehearsal" where the entire class could comment on their performance, the students experienced "first-hand how fundamentally theatre is a collaborative enterprise" (James Bulman and Beth Watkins).

The class, however much it may serve as a window to the outside world, has its own integrity, its own sense of presence. The important thing about bringing other media to the study of Shakespeare, in this case by using what the teacher calls "Shakespeed cards," was that they could be "flipped and played onscreen in class time and then discussed in various ways immediately afterwards also in class time" (Liam Semler).

The contributors also saw themselves as students, learning with and in many cases from their students. Teaching a group of retirees, one professor emeritus found that "Being in a room with people who care a lot about these plays is a high point of my teaching career," and that showing pivotal filmed scenes from Shakespeare to his students "can level the playing field and often elicits reactions that surprise me and make me rethink what I thought I knew" (Alan Dessen). Two teachers who collaborated on a production of *Much Ado About Nothing* with their students learned like students "by seeing the results," and—in a wonderful revelation—one found that she "needed to have more faith in [her] students' good sense" (Fran Teague and Kristin Kundert). The teacher, not as an authority figure in the old sense, not the sole center of attention, not some faceless dispenser of knowledge, but a fellow human being engaged with students—here is how one essayist put this relationship:

Increasingly, I find that I am not so much "delivering" Shakespeare to my heterogeneous and ethnically/racially diverse student populations as I am tapping into what they already know, experientially, in order to clear a path

for them to forge their own connections. I want them to
own what they read, to make it their own.
(Naomi Conn Liebler)

There is a sense of reality, of something physical, alive,
insistent about the theatre that becomes most clear when
we study the playwright with our students. One describes
journeying with his students to encounter "the hard realities
of moving from the potentials of the classroom to the actuals
of the theatre" (Andrew Hartley). One contributor speaks of
these "actuals of the theatre" experienced by the student
as the process by which "students 'enter' a play in which
otherworldly creatures 'vanish,' the dead reappear, a dagger
is imagined hanging in the air, and numerous characters
'vanish' permanently in death" with the result that "stage
directions become more evocative than they initially comprehend" (S. P. Cerasano).

The effect of a good teacher goes beyond the classroom. The student playing Juliet wanted to "live up to [her
teacher's] expectation" in the classroom and onstage, and
confesses that now, seven years later, she can "still feel"
Juliet with her, "like a letter in my pocket" (Jerry Harp and
Erica Terpening), what one essay calls the students' "pride
of ownership of Shakespeare" (James Bulman and Beth
Watkins) in performing his works as extending beyond the
college years.

One of the contributors who works with students both
in the classroom and on stage, a scholar who knows the
life of an actor, speaks of discovering Shakespeare with his
students as like being in "a large country house, a stately
home that one has visited repeatedly, finding a new room or
passage or even a whole wing that one didn't discover on the
last visit" (Russell Jackson).

## Arranging the Essays

In **Section One: Encountering Shakespeare's Verbal
and Visual Text with Students**, the four essayists discuss their work with students in interpreting the plays by

concentrating on what is there on the pages before them. At the same time, all four ask their students to see the text ultimately not as "literature" but as something meant to be performed.

In "Theatricality and the Resistance of Thesis," Andrew Hartley is concerned that students not latch on to a single exclusive reading of the text, and to this end asks them to use experimental, open-ended explorations of the rehearsal technique. Recognizing a plurality of interpretations of a given scene, their focus "is not on what the play as text is but what it might become."

A well-known actor and director, and lecturer, Nick Hutchison in "'That's a Question: How Shall We Try It?' (*The Comedy of Errors*)," encourages his students to apply a "detailed and rigorous" analysis of the text, being especially alert to "cues" in Shakespeare, especially in line and mid-line endings, to raise questions helping them get into a character. Following Peter Hall's "iambic fundamentalist" movement, whose maxim is that while Shakespeare tells you exactly how to say the line, he never tells you "why," Hutchison wants the students to explore the "theatricality" of the text, and to find an answer that "best suits them"—the students, in effect, becoming their own "best teachers."

We recognize that a play is something to be seen as well as heard, a physical entity existing in space and time before an audience. It is significant that in the final weeks of rehearsal, the director will often move about the empty house to get the "look" of the show before various sections of the audience. S. P. Cerasano and Joseph Candido have students focus on this look, how the production's visual dimension complements the words on the page. Cerasano in her "Re-Entering *Macbeth*: 'Witches Vanish' and Other Stage Directions" examines with her students the stage directions in *Macbeth* so that, even in classroom, they can practice "seeing" the text in performance through stage entrances and exits, as well as the blocking of a scene. Among the questions she asks her class is: "Is the ghost of Banquo frightening because it enters ('appears') as a wholly insubstantial entity, or because it is represented as 'half substantial,' existing in a dimension somewhere between what is hazy and what is concrete, connecting the living and the dead?" How do stage directions function symbolically, contributing to the meaning of the play? Joseph Candido in "Seeing the Elizabethan Playhouse in *Richard II*" examines with his students how the Elizabeth playhouse, both physically and symbolically, fleshes out the text and is part of the play's meaning as advanced by Shakespeare's own extraordinary dialogue. Among other moments in that history play, he looks at Richard's dramatic descent from the walls of Flint Castle to encounter Bolingbroke in the base court below (3.3.176–183). How does it work on stage? Later he turns to *The Tempest*, where Shakespeare exploits the "deficiencies" of the Elizabethan stage in order to complement his rich verbal text.

All five essays in **Section Two: Learning through Performance** describe what happens when students actually stage the play, even as their teachers ask them to inform their performances with scholarship on the work (historical, cultural, theatrical, philosophical, aesthetic, and so on).

In "Acting as Ownership in the Shakespeare Classroom," James Bulman and Beth Watkins, husband and wife who are members of the English and Theatre departments respectively, share their experience offering a course in Shakespeare that combined literary study and actor training. Just getting on your feet and doing the play, they realized, is not enough, and so even as they approached Shakespeare through a close reading of the text as well as analysis of actual performances and films, they guided students in thinking of the play as something performative, focusing on everything from the actor's vocal projection to physical gestures that accompany the dialogue. Working with a scene partner, students found open rehearsals especially helpful, where they shared their work with the class and, as a group, considered "the given circumstances, objectives, and obstacles of their characters." To "think and behave as actors" led to some telling insights into the gravediggers' mind-sets in *Hamlet* and into Viola's conflict as she plays a man in *Twelfth Night*. Especially telling are the reactions of students who took this collaboration between the two departments.

In "'Performing *Hamlet*': Repeated Visits to Elsinore," Russell Jackson, who works both in the classroom and onstage, describes the "Performing *Hamlet*" module—he calls it a "semi-practical" module—he has used at the University of Birmingham, where students work in "the rehearsal mode" with short scenes, duplicating the experience of actors and directors. Earlier discussions of scenes available on video led to their using a script prepared ("shortened") for a professional production, the students seeing it as an "open text, rather than from a theoretical or historical standpoint." Without the pressures of a public performance, Jackson's students experience what it is like to mount a production.

I recall in "'Gladly Would He Learn and Gladly Teach': Empowering Students with Shakespeare" how a student, who interrupted what was to be my own generic lecture on *Othello* to argue for a motive for Iago that I had not considered, changed my own reading of the play. Our giving an impromptu class performance of the end of the scene where Iago seduces Othello into vowing to kill Desdemona (3.3) led to my decision to teach Shakespeare through performance in subsequent classes. Students in turn were empowered as actors and directors to make and then enact their own decision on questions such as: to what degree does Gertrude know about or is involved in Claudius's murder of her husband? Or, given the charge, how can they flesh out comic characters, such as the two Dromios in *The Comedy of Errors*, to make them human or real, more than just a repository of jokes and comic action?

The student becomes in part a fellow teacher, and the teacher a fellow student in "Uncertain Text: Student and Teacher Find Their Way Onstage in *Romeo and Juliet*," by Jerry Harp and Erica Terpening. Harp, a college professor, played the Friar and his student Erica Juliet in a production of Shakespeare's tragedy directed by a student. Their relationship in class extended to and influenced their work in the play, where the Friar is the teacher, the "father" to his student's Juliet. Both actors speak of how their real-life friendship as well as events in their separate lives influenced the performance, especially the scenes between the Friar and Juliet, giving a subtext to the two characters that became part of the dramatic world in which Shakespeare situates them.

In "'In Practice Let Us Put It Presently': Learning with *Much Ado*," Fran Teague of the University of Georgia's English Department and Kristin Kundert of that school's Department of Theatre analyze their collaboration in a production of Shakespeare's comedy. They describe what happened both in class and onstage, where their students worked as dramaturgs, researchers, in-rehearsal evaluators, and actors. Teague speaks of what she herself learned from her students during rehearsals, and Kundert, wanting to create a world that was large and dramatic, containing the possibility for big emotions, design, and music, relied on her colleague and "50 students and faculty [who] worked on the show," one that, as she adds, was seen by over 1,500 people.

**Section Three: Approaching Shakespeare from Some Specific Angles** examines four instances of what happens when teachers employ a technological device, isolate a specific feature of the performance script, employ a teaching strategy, or ask their students to take into account the actual medium in which Shakespeare wrote. Common to all four is that the teachers find an angle to get their students into the plays.

In "Shakespeeding into *Macbeth* and *The Tempest*: Teaching with the Shakespeare Reloaded Website," Liam Semler uses randomly organized short video clips hidden behind online flip cards to provoke novel approaches to teaching the plays. Some of the flip cards lead to video content directly related to the play under discussion, while other flip cards suggest unrelated content that triggers surprising connections and insights. The flip cards are his way of responding "to the digital revolution which is transforming not only the educational landscape, but also the neural landscape inside students' heads." Semler discusses the education philosophy of and then provides students' reactions to what he calls "the gamified learning module."

In "'And So Everyone According to His Cue': Practice-led Teaching and Cue-scripts in the Classroom," Miranda

Fay Thomas in her work with students at London's Globe Theatre uses a cue script, where each actor is given not the complete play but only his or her character's lines with cues, as a way of letting students experience the play the way Shakespeare's actors did in rehearsal. Her goals are for students to see the drama from a practical rather than a wholly literary perspective and to teach them about early acting styles. She offers, for example, that scene in *The Merchant of Venice* where Salarino and Antonio use their cues—Antonio's "at his request" and Salarino's "my bond"—to force the actor playing Shylock to speak over them. Her students thereby consider the dramatic tension created not only among the three characters but among the actors themselves. The students learn more about Shakespeare's own performance text and "the theatrical context" from which the characters emerge.

In "Collaborating with Shakespeare," Frederick Kiefer helps his students get into the play by asking them as a "creative option" to the standard course paper to write scenes in prose that expand or comment on particular moments in Shakespeare's text—"extra" scenes, additions to the story, so that the student playwrights become collaborators with Shakespeare. For example, he asks them to write a new scene appearing at the end of act 3 in *The Merchant of Venice*. They are to imagine that Shylock and Jessica meet after she has fallen in love with and married Lorenzo. He asks the students to consider the emotional dynamics of such an encounter. What has led the characters to make the decisions that so profoundly change their lives? What caused the split between father and daughter in the first place? Was Shylock remiss as a father and, if so, did his behavior engender Jessica's disaffection? Could Jessica's decision to abandon her community have something to do with her sense of jeopardy in Venetian society? For Kiefer, such questions, far from moving readers away from the script, paradoxically take them further *into* the world of the play. He offers examples of student responses to the assignment which he found a joy to read.

In "Shakespeare Without Print," Paul Menzer shows what happens when students "read" Shakespeare through "digitalized, oral, or reconstructed manuscript interfaces," his argument being that our present printed text confines students of Shakespeare to a medium "in which [the playwright] did not traffic." Breaking down, or, away from the printed text, seeing it in parts rather than as a single printed document, "alienates students from their familiar encounters," and can, in Menzer's words, lead to "productive discoveries in the classroom."

**Section Four: Shakespeare in Various Classrooms** records four of the numerous ways in which teachers in different settings have engaged their students. What happens in each classroom is influenced by the nature of the students, their backgrounds, and the personality and, perhaps even more, the principles of the teacher, as well as the world outside the classroom as it impinges on both students and their teacher.

In "'That Depends: What Do You Want Two Plus Two to Be?': Teaching Possibility," Cary Mazer compares and contrasts what happens in three Shakespeare courses he offers: Acting Shakespeare, Dramaturgy, and a seminar on Shakespeare Performance History. In Acting Shakespeare, he uses the Stanislavski principle that a character's energy is impelled by objectives and that the actor plays the character not by attempting to feel an emotion but by having the same objectives. In Dramaturgy, students select a five-play season for a hypothetical theatre company and then make decisions on everything from the theatre's mission and target audience to cutting the script—even where to put the intermission. In Shakespeare Performance History, students explore the aesthetics of reception and how the ways that audiences perceive and interpret meaning are specific to time and place. Still, each course asks some basic questions: what does the play mean? How does the play work? What, finally, *is* the play? As he recounts how students in each handled the assignments, he finds that the answers vary, predictably, according to the course, even as the shift in emphasis from meaning to how the text "works" onstage remain constant.

In "'Who's There?' 'Nay, Answer Me. Stand and Unfold Yourself': Attending to Students in Diversified Settings,"

Naomi Conn Liebler describes how she helped students in the inner city and in middle and secondary schools "forge their own connections" with *Romeo and Juliet*. Liebler also tells of a graduate student who came to her with questions about race in *Othello* and later became supervisor for English education for the district. She offers examples of how students bring their lives and experiences to their study of Shakespeare, making it an unpredictably rich experience, regardless of the "level" of the class. She also discusses a section on the Teaching Shakespeare/Shakespeare for Teachers workshops offered at Montclair State University to include both inner-city and middle and secondary school classes.

Patrick Hart in "Unpicking the Turkish Tapestry: Teaching Shakespeare in Anatolia" describes what it is like teaching Shakespeare in a country ruled by an oppressive government and beset with the tensions of an Ottoman and specifically Muslim culture challenged by a culturally laden, even neo-colonial, imposition. He then describes a student project that tried to contain or navigate these political and cultural tensions: a silent film adaptation of act 3 scene 1 of *Measure for Measure*, where students could explore current attitudes toward women but in an art form that allowed them to downplay the value of western cultural models and inspirations. Other students filmed the final scene of *Hamlet* in the style of an episode from one of the TV shows set at the Ottoman court and wildly popular across the Middle East.

Alan Dessen in "Teaching Shakespeare to Retirees in the OLLI Program" reviews his own extraordinary career as a teacher–scholar, from the large lecture courses he gave as a TA, to working for 45 years with undergraduate and graduate students, to the course he now gives in Shakespeare for fellow retirees. He examines the challenges, even the disadvantages, as well as the advantages of working with older students who outside the classroom have families, professions, and "who bring life experiences to their study of the plays." Dessen recounts his experience and the reactions of his "retired" students to his use of video, DVDs, and the BBC Shakespeare series to bring performance into their classroom. At the end of his essay he comments: "I have no idea how long this final phase will last ... and at the end of the day after a 90-minute class I sometimes feel brain-dead. Still, if the in-class adrenalin keeps kicking in, I hope to continue. In Touchstone's words: 'much virtue in *if*.'"

In **Afterword**: "Cur Non?", June Schlueter filters the basic issues raised in the collection's 17 essays, responding as they do to the questions of how and why we teach Shakespeare, through her account of the life of Professor Francis March (1825–1911) of Lafayette College. March is thought to have been the first college teacher in the United States to include a Shakespeare play on his syllabus. A scholar of the Classics and a philologist, he adopted the motto of the Marquis de Lafayette after whom his college was named: "Cur Non?" (Why not?) in asking why can't Shakespeare's plays be studied "after the same methods as Homer and Demosthenes?" In his *Method of Philological Study of the English Language*, he presented his analysis of act 1 scene 1 of *Julius Caesar*, and took this same detailed linguistic scholarship to his work with students. As Schlueter observes, his "method of teaching Shakespeare may no longer be viable, but it is hard not to admire the mastery of detail and the breadth of knowledge the discipline of philology demanded." But March also asked students larger questions about Shakespeare's works: what lessons [are they] intended to teach? What conspiracies in England during the life of Shakespeare influenced the playwright? Such questions and the concomitant multiple understandings are, surely, how Shakespeare got into the curriculum in the first place. As Schlueter observes, "the impulse to question" informs the teaching, in various ways, of the contributors to this present collection. I spoke earlier of the closed door to the classroom, and, appropriately, the Afterword concludes with "Whatever the impact of philology on teaching today, twenty-first-century Shakespeareans can be grateful to Francis March for having opened his classroom door to Shakespeare and for asking 'Cur Non?'"

This collection was never meant to be a "how to." As you will see from these essays, the how and why emerge distinctly in every instance. The confluence of Shakespeare, student, and teacher fits each teacher's component precisely because the study of Shakespeare allows it and encourages it. As a whole, what other works show such plasticity that they can retain their integrity in almost any manner of interpretation? A living playwright might put restrictions on his works. Fortunately for us, Shakespeare cannot.

## Notes

1 G. B. Shands, ed., *Teaching Shakespeare: Passing It On* (Malden, MA: Wiley-Blackwell, 2009). See also: *Rex Gibson, Teaching Shakespeare: A Handbook for Teachers* (Cambridge: Cambridge University Press, 1998); H. R. Corsen, *Teaching Shakespeare with Film and Television: A Guide* (Westport, CT: Greenwood Press, 1997); Richard M. Adams, *Teaching Shakespeare: Essays on Approaches to Shakespeare in Schools and Colleges* (London: Robert Royce, 1985); Ayanna Thompson, *Teaching Shakespeare with Purpose: A Student-Centred Approach* (London: Bloomsbury, 2016).

2 See entries at: www.google.com/search?q=Teaching+Shakespeare&ie=utf-8&oe=utf-8&client=firefox-b-ab (accessed June 16, 2018).

3 Elizabeth Redden, "The Changing English Major," January 11, 2017, at: www.insidehighered.com/news/2017/01/11/amid-enrollment-declines-speakers-consider-shape-english-major (accessed June 16, 2018).

4 Kent Cartwright, quoted in Redden.

5 Peter J. Kalliney, "We Reversed Our Declining English Enrollment: Here's How," *Chronicle of Higher Education*, April 2, 2018, at: www.chronicle.com/article/We-Reversed-Our-Declining/243009 (accessed June 16, 2018).

6 Sheila Slaughter and Gary Rhoades, *Academic Capitalism and the New Economy* (Baltimore: John Hopkins University Press, 2004).

7 Frank Donoghue, *The Last Professors: The Corporate University and the Fate of the Humanities* (New York: Fordham University Press, 2008).

8 And see: Gerald Graff's *Professing Literature: An Institutional History* (Chicago: University of Chicago Press, 1987); Benjamin Ginsberg, *The Fall of the Faculty: The Rise of the All-Administrative University And Why It Matters* (Oxford: Oxford

University Press, 2011); James F. English, *The Global Future of English Studies* (Malden, MA: Wiley-Blackwell, 2012); Evan Watkins, *Work Time* (Stanford: Stanford University Press, 1989); John Guillory, *Cultural Capital: The Problem of Literary Canon Formation* (Chicago and London: University of Chicago Press, 1993); Marc Bousquet, *How the University Works* (New York: New York University Press, 2008); Maggie Berg and Barbara K. Seeber, *The Slow Professor: Challenging the Culture of Speed in the Academy* (Toronto: University of Toronto Press, 2016); Ayanna Thompson, *Teaching Shakespeare with Purpose: A Student-Centred Approach* (London: Bloomsbury, 2016).

# SECTION ONE

Encountering
Shakespeare's Verbal and
Visual Text with Students

Encountering
Shakespeare's Verbal and
Visual Text with Students

# 1

# Theatricality and the Resistance of Thesis

## *Andrew James Hartley*

When I was a PhD student in the Boston University English department in the early fourteenth century, I was given the opportunity to take a break from my usual teaching duties to serve as a Teaching Assistant in a script analysis class in the theatre department. They were shorthanded and I had directed a couple of times for a student theatre group, so it seemed like a good match.

It wasn't.

I butted heads with the students over their writing and their approach to scripts, particularly over their failure to justify performance choices through textual evidence. In one class, a student—baffled rather than defiant—observed that I kept hitting them with "why?" questions. Why were they giving a character this accent or physicality; why did they want to set the production in this particular period; why did they think this musical underscoring would work during this scenic transition. "Exactly," I said, feeling like I was finally getting through.

"It's interesting," said the student. "We're always taught to ask 'why not?'"

It was a profound moment, one that should have taught me something significant. It did, eventually, but only after years of working in professional theatre as a dramaturg and gradually figuring out the disciplinary difference indicated by the student's observation. As someone with a background in literary study I had been taught that the text was the origin point of all meaning, even if that origin point was shaded by historical factors which demanded that I look beyond the text and into the original cultural moment from which it emerged in order to understand that text. The theatre student had been taught to treat the text as a jumping-off point, the inciting incident of their own creative journey. In her view it was generally assumed that what resulted should be in accord with the text (though even that could be fudged through alteration and adaptation) but that what might happen on stage was infinitely possible, the end product being something new, not the enacting of something that preexisted it.

This is, of course, old news to those who practice any form of performance criticism, and has become central to serious thought about the staging of Shakespeare since the mid nineties, thanks in part to W. B. Worthen, but the primacy of text can be a hard habit to break. Even when scholars concede the way in which theatre necessarily constructs stage meaning which is extra-textual, it is especially hard to shelve another of literary studies' primary mandates, the impulse to univocality and argument. In my English classes, for instance, I constantly wrestle with the implicit paradox of my own course structure where, on the one hand, I try to open up the plays we are studying to multiple interpretations, but end the semester requiring what most of us demand: a thesis-driven paper. Students are asked to produce what we as scholars are used to thinking of as the core scholarly unit of our field: a textual analysis which makes a compelling case for a particular reading of the play, one which badgers and banishes all contrary elements and the critics who have voiced them, in pursuit of that most hallowed of scholarly objects, an essay which is closely attentive to the text while being single-minded in its focus, clear in its exposition, and so logical in its conclusions that, at least for a time, the reader is convinced that no contrary position is intellectually viable. The result is a kind of critical unicorn, beautiful, elegant, and pointed.

Like said unicorn, it is also an exercise in fantasy and wish-fulfillment.

We know that Shakespeare's plays sustain multiple interpretations, which is part of what makes them Shakespeare, and that those interpretations are subject to individual interpretation and evolution over time, yet we persist in demanding that our students pretend, at least for the duration of a paper, that one interpretative approach trumps all others.

However critical I am of such a strategy, the opposite extreme is at least as problematic, and we have all seen productions which have been incoherent, unproductively random, and self-contradictory. Theatre professionals like to fasten onto the question of whether a moment or an approach "works" on stage, but that is a highly debatable standard, used too often to dodge "intellectual" criticism. The literary "why?" is no worse than the theatrical "why not?" if the resultant production fails to satisfy, intrigue, stimulate, or otherwise function as an engaging piece of theatre.

For several years now we at the University of North Carolina (UNC) Charlotte have been bringing the Notre Dame-based Actors From The London Stage (AFTLS) company to campus. I always ensure that the play to be staged is part of my class syllabi in both English and theatre, usually contriving to arrange that we have spent several class sessions on the play before the company arrives, allowing one class for the actors to work with the students and one more class to debrief after the students have seen the production. In 2011, AFTLS brought what was, to my mind, a very successful production of *The Tempest*. As with all their stagings, the company worked with only five actors and no designated director.

Of course, it is virtually impossible to teach *The Tempest* these days without foregrounding colonial issues, and I find that discussion of race, conquest, and otherness is an excellent angle for getting students to connect and grapple with the play. This is particularly true at UNC Charlotte, where the student body is more diverse than most and which is comparatively close to the site of the Jamestown colony, giving an extra sense of proximity to one of the grounding myths of the play's origins. The discourse of slavery surrounding Caliban and, to a lesser extent, Ariel, the question of what constitutes humanity in the play, the framing of the exotic and foreign, all have special potency and relevance in the classroom, where recent history and contemporary notions of racial politics are especially urgent.

The AFTLS production, however, was all white, a fact which surprised, shocked, and even offended some of the students. Much of the discourse of colonialism which had dominated our classroom discussions was at best muted in a staging which seemed uninterested in race, feeling like a throwback to pre-1970s productions in this respect, though it retained a less-than-Victorian skepticism about Prospero himself, particularly since the actor (Dale Rapley) also played his unrepentant brother, Antonio. The most memorable aspect of the show was surely the physicality of Ariel, whose magic was seemingly wound up by her running around the playing space at speed. Lacking the bells and whistles of more complex productions and design elements, the show focused on the actor–audience relationship. As is often the case with AFTLS, the production emphasized the bodies, voices, and skillsets of the actors, privileging in-scene relationship/character work over more clearly signposted "concept" productions. Macro readings were harder to see, so that the univocality or thesis of the show inhered more in its methodology than in its "take" on the play.

The students were put in the position of having to either jettison their preconceptions about what the play was essentially *about*, or construct a historically untenable argument about why the play on stage should always center on actors of color. The resulting conversation was productively troubled as they had to navigate what it means in the twenty-first century not to play *The Tempest* as being about race and colonialism, and to consider what the resulting production *was* about. The show clearly worked, even if it wasn't the show we had been expecting. This discussion also served to problematize the binary either/or of colonial approach versus non-colonial approach, generating instead a series of questions about what emerges from a play when certain elephants are removed from the room. This in turn led to a more theoretical conversation about the relationship between text and performance, pushing back against the moralistic imperative to play a given reading as the only viable alternative. What is a production of *The Tempest* if it is wholly divorced from racial issues? Is it necessarily conservative, a dodge of the colonial baggage hung like a millstone around the play's neck, affirming instead older humanist universals in ways that are, in that most academically mealy-mouthed of phrases, problematic?

On the other hand, might such a production challenge a received wisdom about the play which has become theatrically stultifying, finding avenues for the text to become surprising and dynamic, even subversive? I teach the play as being about colonialism, but it was liberating to have my expectations thwarted in ways that demanded I listen to the characters and let them dictate the terms of the production.

AFTLS have to be booked months in advance, so it is impossible to know what you are going to get until the company arrives, a fact potentially exacerbated by the directorless method.[1] In advance of their visits. I confess to some anxiety about this. While I was pleased with the *Tempest* production, it generated in talkbacks with the cast some familiar actor rhetoric against political readings which supposedly "flatten out" the play. The cast's bafflement about US expectations of a racialized production sometimes took the form of a very British "post-racial" universalism which, while well-meant, I never find especially convincing.[2] Prior to booking their 2013 *Othello* tour, I reached out to the company to ensure that the lead role would be played by an actor of color—it was—though I still found the production oddly unselfconscious about the show's racial politics. The cast remarked, for instance, that certain racial epithets had been cut from the (generally very full) script because the actors were not comfortable saying them, a decision which—while well-intentioned—seriously compromised the production, rendering the racial issue at the play's heart a kind of incidental concern. I should add that such moments are quintessentially teachable and generate productive discussion, again, about what it is we are doing when we take the infinite possibilities we glimpse in the text and make finite choices on stage. Even when I dislike a choice, it has proved generative in getting students—especially literature students—to engage with the hard realities of moving from the potentials of the classroom to the actuals of the theatre.

The AFTLS is frequently described as "actor-centered"—apparently on the understanding that that is a good thing, dodging as it does overblown design elements and directorial meddling and instead re-grounding the work in text, body, and voice. I'm wary of the mysticism which tends to result from such assumptions, of course, and fear a certain anti-intellectualism in the surrounding rhetoric, so that, directors and designers notwithstanding, the person whose work I really miss in such shows is the dramaturg who might force more intellectual cohesion from the production. Because actor-centered doesn't merely describe a condition of rehearsal. It contains an ideological bias toward the granular over the macro, the finely sharpened pencil over the bold brushstroke, and the assumption that what matters most about the play is story as encapsulated by the conscious choices of the cast. This is particularly true in Shakespeare, where the injunction to be "in the moment," to think and react on and in the line and otherwise be in what Patsy Rodenburg calls the "state of readiness," privileges impulse and psychological reaction over large-scale political mapping (usually characterized as overlaying) which, it is argued, reduces the actors and, by extension, the characters to puppets serving some directorially scripted agenda.

Dale Rapley's thinking about playing Prospero for AFTLS is a case in point:

> For the action of the play, what matters most is that Prospero is a brother and a father. Fundamentally, this is a family drama with political significance. He is also a scholar, a thinker, a philosopher, a pusher of boundaries, a conjuror, an outsider, a Renaissance man in all senses. We learn early on that he has left the political stuff to

his brother, while he concentrates on his studies. He is
the perennial student. He believes the people love him
dearly, but seems to have no desire to take political
responsibility for them, preferring, instead, to spend
time in his library, leaving state affairs under the control
of his brother. I couldn't help thinking, how well did he
know his brother? How developed is his awareness of
the character of others? Is he one of these cold, bookish,
emotionally stunted men, who doesn't recognize any need
for much human contact? In any case, was such neglect of
his dukedom wise? Does he really want to be Duke? […]

Prospero has taken Caliban under his wing, the
only creature he discovered on the island with a "human
shape", taught him how to speak and used him as his odd
job man … But with … the recent attempt by Caliban
to have his carnal way with [Miranda], Prospero has
been forced to throw Caliban out of the house, confining
him to a rock and consequently creating an enemy of
growing resentment that can only be controlled by threats
of supernatural torture. Is Prospero, then, a tyrant, a
colonizer, riding roughshod over the will and ways of the
indigenous population? Or is he simply a protective father,
taking all the steps necessary to protect his daughter's
virginity, not only for the sake of her emotional and
physical well being, but also bearing in mind her future as
a possible Queen of Naples. For me the prime determinant
of his behavior must be the latter, however misguided
Prospero's attempt at civilising—at nurturing—the
gullible "deformed slave" Caliban may be. Later on we see
Caliban's pitiful need to be led by Stephano, the drunken
butler. Whatever our western colonialist perspective,
I think the power struggle between Prospero and Caliban
only really emerges after that thwarted sexual act. There
is no sense that Caliban was previously unhappy to have
Prospero as his master—and Miranda as his companion—
however unjust we may see it from our enlightened
twenty-first century point of view.

We encountered a lot of resistance on tour to our—
that is, the cast's—belief that the play is not mainly a

play about colonialism. I believe the issue is certainly present but that the play deals, among other things, fundamentally with how we allow ourselves to be ruled at all. That said, when approaching a part my main questions stem from "why is my character doing this or that?" Any political motive, seems to me always to come from a personal, psychological imperative.

(Rapley, 2012)

The "basics" for Rapley are entirely about relationships. Here and elsewhere in his article he stays away from moral judgment of the characters in his attempt to find their inner logic and what makes them interesting. Most clearly, he avoids macro political readings as antithetical to his work of finding the truth of the character in that moment-to-moment consciousness he wishes to create on stage, so that—as he concludes above—any political motivation is small, immediate, and psychologically driven. I should add that Rapley's social media presence reveals him to be a deeply political person, left of center and alert to social and economic issues. So the side-stepping of the colonial in *The Tempest* seems to me a feature of an expressly humanistic actor training, one which sees the core truth of the play as grounded in textually based character relationships, all of which fits the AFTLS mandate perfectly.

The paradox here is that both our literature students and the AFTLS actors believe that what they are doing originates in the text. The problem is that they don't read the text in the same way, and while I may seem skeptical of Rapley's commentary on who Prospero is, I'm equally skeptical of our students' (equally preconditioned; *trained*, in fact) baseline assumption that the heart of all Shakespeare plays is their engagement with political issues, and identity politics in particular. While there are times when I want to see a directorial or dramaturgical hand in an AFTLS production, I find the effect of shaking the students out of their political complacency helpful, forcing them to reconsider the plays in less schematic terms.

This year's AFTLS visit revolved around their production of *Measure for Measure*. It came at the height of the media storm around revelations concerning Harvey Weinstein and other notables engaged in a widespread culture of sexual harassment and intimidation which generated the #MeToo movement. My classes prior to the theatre company's visit were charged once more with a sense of Shakespeare's political relevance. I could not have anticipated just how topical this play would become when we committed to their residency, nor had I any idea what the production would do with the issues of the play or how they would resolve the vexed question of how to stage Isabella's response to the Duke's final marriage proposal. I have seen productions which attempted to pass the moment off as jokey or romantic (as similar productions might attempt to dodge the mines scattered around the ending of *The Taming of the Shrew*) and I was anxious not that the production wouldn't be teachable, but that it would look intellectually flimsy, tone deaf, or complicit in the very oppression we had been discussing in the classroom.

It didn't, or not quite. The handling of Angelo and the nightmare scenario which generates Isabella's painfully prescient "To whom should I complain?" speech was pretty well handled, though the actor playing Angelo tried hard to render his character's villainy as a kind of social retardation turned monstrous rather than an absolute evil (a reading which fails to take into account his prior dealings with Mariana). Actors often try to understand their characters, to connect with them, even to like them, and while that is understandable and makes a kind of Stanislavskian sense, finding nuance and complexity in what might otherwise be (again) "flat" moralism, it does not sit well with students whose sense of character is frequently driven primarily by plot and imagining themselves therein, as overlaid by certain political truisms.

Our classroom discussion of the Duke had pushed toward the Machiavellian, seeing him as using the action of the play, particularly the final scene, to cement his own power by making everyone else dependent on his restoration of order. This had been countered to a lesser extent by older readings of the Duke as a semi-divine presence motivated by benevolence, understanding, and justice. What we got in the AFTLS production, however, was neither. This Duke was manic, volatile, and borderline unstable. He was socially awkward to the point of being on the autism spectrum, and he was both entirely unselfconscious and passionate. His odd decisions were all conceived and acted upon impulsively and without forethought, so that the audience was confronted not by a Machiavelli or a figure of providential sanctity, but by a confused and almost childlike figure who was, quite literally, making it up as he went along. As with the *Tempest* production, the choice fixated on character "in the moment," operating on the assumption (again, à la Rodenburg) that what isn't expressly scripted is insignificant, while denying the possibility of characters lying to the audience or even to themselves.[3] While my students saw the Duke as a Machiavel playing a long game and setting each beat of the story up in order to create its end, the AFTLS actors gave us a series of snap decisions whose motivation was largely unreadable and lost in socially awkward character depths. There was no sense that this Duke knew Mariana existed before she became integral to the plot, and his final punishment of Lucio came out of deep pathological hurt rather than political expedience. Again, the interpretation muted the play's political edge a little, but worked in character terms, at least for this production and for a certain model of what theatre is.

And that is surely the value of exposing students to performance. They are forced to shed the thesis-driven approach to drama and to recognize the form's essential pliability, its capacity to be something other than it appears on the page without violating that page, and its nature as something fundamentally plural. The Duke might not have been the Duke I would have wanted, played, or directed, but it was a viable Duke, one whose logic was determined by the parameters of the show in front of us. Such stagings and an intellectual engagement with them break down those limiting assumptions behind students who talk about seeing "the movie" of a play, as if there can only be one. As such, the value of even the most limited production is as a challenge to the assumption that a show should manifest that thesis-driven sense of textual meaning, revealing instead a sense of a play's complex theatrical potentialities.

## Notes

1 The show is reviewed by program staff and tweaks suggested before the tour begins, but it is not clear how extensive such tweaks are. It should also be said that five actors and no director really means five directors.
2 I love the diversity of British television, for instance, but find the refusal of such shows to actually engage with issues of race disingenuous.
3 Rodenburg's actorly analysis of Hal's first-act soliloquy in I Henry IV in *Speaking Shakespeare* is a study in this kind of thinking, presenting what my students would read as the reveal of the deception he has been playing throughout the scene ("I know you all ...") as an in-the-moment realization, a plan which comes to him as he speaks. I'm wary of such trusting of the character and text, the way it limits actor choice and implies the correctness of some interpretations, though I recognize that actors have to embrace the logic of what they are doing. That such an approach makes an actor more honest on stage, however, seems to me highly debatable.

## References

Rapley, Dale. *The Tempest for iPad*. Elliott Visconsi's Luminary Digital Media company in partnership with The Folger Shakespeare Library and Simon & Schuster, February 2012.
Rodenburg, Patsy. *Speaking Shakespeare*. Palgrave/Macmillan, 2002.

# 2

# "That's a Question: How Shall We Try It?" (*The Comedy of Errors*)

## *Nick Hutchison*

My experience teaching Shakespeare is fundamentally similar to my other job of directing Shakespeare in professional theatre: I am mostly employed to direct students either in scenes or in a workshop environment, occasionally in a whole play, but never in a classroom. My work therefore tends to be practical rather than theoretical—on its feet, not around a table. However, as a fully paid-up member of the late, great Peter Hall's "Iambic Fundamentalist" movement, I teach students the clues that Shakespeare gives the actors to illuminate character, to direct them in a Renaissance theatrical world where rehearsal was minimal, just as I would with professional actors. I do this largely through a detailed and rigorous reading of the text, especially the verse form, acknowledging line endings, mid-line endings, and all the other technical clues that the writer offers the actor, working in a similar way to Hall and Giles Block at the Globe.

However, I am also a great believer in Hall's maxim that while Shakespeare tells you exactly how to say the line, he never tells you "why." I stress to my students that what I am doing is making sure they know the questions to ask, even though the answers will vary from production to production, director to director, actor to actor. The important thing is spotting where there is a question and trying, in rehearsal, to find the best way to answer it; otherwise you are just skating, however elegantly, across the surface of the text. Only by working theatrically with the text will you find the answer that best suits you. In this, I hope I am educating rather than teaching. I try to empower the student to find their own answers to the questions that the playwright asks, and to realize that there is never going to be a single correct response and that that fluidity is where the joy lies in working with these scripts, that they provide endless possibilities and therefore infinite pleasure.

I approach the text with an increasing specificity of questioning, starting with the larger, more general questions and honing them down to the microscopic. In this way I hope to enthuse students with the very precise approach that I believe gives texture to a performance.[1]

For a modern Shakespearean actor, the most familiar way of working out character is clearly from the context of the play and the character's situation within it: "I respond like this to this situation, so what does that tell me about who I am?" When Feste in the brief opening to act 3 scene 2 of *Twelfth Night* responds to Cesario's patronizing "I warrant thou art a merry fellow and car'st for nothing" with the dismissive "Not so, Sir, I do care for something, but in my conscience, Sir, I do not care for you," it is essential for the actor to ask himself not just why he doesn't care for Cesario, but, more importantly, what it is he does care for, and how this impacts on the character as a whole. Add to that the question of why he addresses Cesario as "sir" 17 times in a scene of only 38 lines, and it is clear that the scene is infinitely more complex than it at first appears. As always, the specific answer will depend on performer, director, and production, but an actor who fails to address these questions is not fully investing in the character, and this will leave an audience short-changed, watching a cipher, not a fully fledged person.

These contextual decisions are also clear with a character like Sir Toby. Ask most students to describe him and their first point will be that he is a drunk: a very funny drunk, albeit with a streak of cruelty visible in his treatment of Aguecheek and Malvolio. An actor cannot just leave it there, though; to fully inhabit the role his first question has to be, "Why do I drink?" "What is it that drives Toby to the bottle?" Once that question is asked, the answer is clear from the context of the play. We know that Toby is Olivia's uncle, and his place in the household suggests that he is her father's brother. As Olivia's father was until his death, Toby must be the younger brother, so he is in the invidious position of being the back-up to his older brother, the "heir and spare" syndrome we still see in the British Royal Family today. His role is to step in if anything happens to his brother. However, as soon as Olivia's elder brother was born, the title skipped down a generation, and Toby's purpose in life evaporated; he has almost no chance of being called on to inherit the title, and therefore no role in the household. From Jane Austen to Sebastian Flyte, we can see the problem of younger brothers in the aristocracy run throughout literature and documentary history. Toby drinks because there is no need not to, and one can see in his casual cruelty and maudlin sentiment the typical traits of the alcoholic.

Of course, the questions asked by students can also relate to and challenge established theory or tradition, and blow the cobwebs out of your mind in the process. The student actor playing Celia in *As You Like It* at the McCoy Theatre at Rhodes College, Memphis, delivered the opening of act 3 scene 4, the jocular discussion between the two cousins of Orlando's sincerity in love, as if she were playing one of those dark scenes in Strindberg. When I pointed out that it was customary (and therefore "right") to play this as playful banter with her love-sick cousin while they wait for Orlando to show up, she responded, "I just can't see where it says '*jokingly*' in my script." In a spirit of grudging cooperation, we tried it her way, and—damn her eyes!—it changed the whole scene, and the play, for the infinitely better. Rosalind's attempts to woo Orlando as Ganymede became as much a trial to prove Celia wrong in her mistrust of his emotions as a love-game, and it made the relationship between the women so much more textured, and the stakes much higher. I always tell students that their answers might change how I see a play: I don't think they ever believe me, but it is true.

However, it is the specific textual questions that really
interest me; sometimes, of course, these relate to editorial decisions over the centuries rather than specifics
in Shakespeare's text. In act 5 scene 4 of *Much Ado About
Nothing*, editors since Theobald have given the line "Peace,
I will stop your mouth" to Benedick (a practice thankfully
now changing). Students always comment on how this gives
him the final word, that he silences Beatrice, and how wrong
this feels. I point out that in both the Quarto and the Folio
it is Leonato's line, so once you've removed Theobald's stage
direction of "kissing her," how does this work on stage? Every
permutation I've explored ends up with Leonato pushing
the lovers' heads together, meaning that they end as equals,
forced at last to finally stop being witty and actually kiss.

However, the text always tells you the answers to seek, if
you know what to ask. Beatrice and Benedick are frequently
understood as mirror images of each other, the male and
female embodiments of wit, but closer inspection of the play
shows that this is not how Shakespeare writes them. When
Ursula and Hero gull her into love, Beatrice's response is
movingly heartfelt:

> What fire is in mine ears? Can this be true?
> Stand I condemned for pride and scorn so much?
> Contempt, farewell; and maiden pride, adieu.
> No glory lives behind the back of such.
> And, Benedick, love on. I will requite thee,
> Taming my wild heart to thy loving hand
> If thou dost love, my kindness shall incite thee
> To bind our loves up in a holy band.
>
> (3.1.107–114)[2]

This scene occurs deep into the show, and these are her
first lines of verse. It is a theatrical (if not academic) given
that verse tends to be the language of the heart, rather than
the prosaic language of the head. Beatrice's speech, therefore, indicates that, on falling in love and appreciating the
implications of the scornful persona she has adopted, she
shifts her language from the head (the carapace of wit she

has employed up to this point) to a language more directly from the heart. We, the audience, understand what has just happened to her as much from how she speaks as from what she speaks; even if we are precisely unaware of the prose-to-verse shift, we sense the change in her language and her persona.

Benedick, however, responds to his gulling (by a very inept group of tricksters) very differently:

> This can be no trick. The conference was sadly borne
> ... Love me! Why, it must be requited. I hear how I am
> censured. They say I will bear myself proudly if I perceive
> the love come from her. ... They say the lady is fair. 'Tis
> a truth, I can bear them witness. And virtuous—'tis so,
> I cannot reprove it. And wise, but for loving me. By my
> troth, it is no addition to her wit—nor no great argument
> of her folly, for I will be horribly in love with her.
>
> (2.3.209–223)

Unlike Beatrice's speech, Benedick's remains firmly in prose, in the language of the head, and it is clear that his decision to be "horribly in love" is just that, a decision, not an emotional response. Whereas Beatrice listens to the reports of others and responds emotionally, by "taming" her "wild heart" to his "loving hand," Benedick weighs the pros and cons. My questions to the student actor are: what does this tell us about the two characters, what differences does it make to the overall performance of character that the two protagonists respond in such a way, and how do you make that tally with the rest of the play? I know my answers to these questions, but, knowing that theirs might be different, I have to accept that difference.

One of the joys about working like this with students is that it can lead to a completely new interpretation of a scene: if you play the specific, not the general, it can become a very different beast from that suggested by a merely sur-face understanding. I frequently use the Hamlet/Ophelia "nunnery" scene in act 3 scene 1 to illustrate this. Students at first reading are always quick to berate Hamlet for chauvinism, sexism, and bullying, which is, of course, a possible interpretation. There is always at least one student who leaps to inform me that "nunnery" is a euphemism for a brothel, thus compounding Hamlet's guilt, and so we can safely dismiss a four-hour play as the justifiable demise of a seventeenth-century Harvey Weinstein. However, if you break the scene down and ask specific questions, I think it becomes something very different.

You start by analyzing who is speaking verse and who prose. How does that change, and who changes it? You ask what they call each other (fair, nymph, thou vs you, mine honoured Lord, etc). You look at the first half of the scene and ask who Hamlet is insulting (himself almost exclusively), and you then query the pivotal moment of the scene. To Hamlet's "Where's your father?" Ophelia replies, "At home, my Lord."

I ask why Hamlet suddenly breaks off his self-deprecating rant to ask this, why Ophelia lies—and, indeed, if she does—and how that choice affects our view of her. I then get the students to examine closely how the language changes after that point: why does every one of Ophelia's lines begin with the theatrical "O"; why does Hamlet suddenly become so vicious? What implications might this have? We then stage it bearing all this in mind, and another interpretation becomes very clear: I stress that it's not the "right" interpretation, just that it is a possible one ... that this scene emphasizes their togetherness, not its polar opposite.

The joy of close textual questioning is that one never stops digging for clues, for the choices the text forces one to make. As mentioned above, you start with wide-ranging general character decisions, but then the microscope zooms in and the verse structure in all its detail becomes significant. The mid-line ending, and shared half lines, offer up a huge scope for textual interpretation, and this is likely to be work most students have never been asked to do. In act 5 scene 2 of *Love's Labour's Lost*, Katherine suddenly dampens the satirical mood by recalling her late sister, killed by Cupid, dead of a broken heart:

> He made her melancholy, sad and heavy,
> And so she died. Had she been light, like you,
> Of such a merry nimble stirring spirit,
> She might have been a grandam ere she died ...

She breaks out of her sad recollection to engage in some pyro-technic wordplay with Rosaline, but what interests me, and throws up a number of possibilities, is that mid-line turn-around which is frequently played: "And so she died. *(Pause for a whole load of acting as she tries to pull it together)* ... Had she been light, like you ..."

But the mid-line ending means that there is no pause; it is an immediate change of thought. Students have to ask them-selves how this works, and what it tells us about Katherine that she can go from gloomy retrospection to verbal fencing in a heartbeat. As always, there are a number of perfectly valid answers, but only if you know to ask the question.

A similar moment happens in act 3 scene 2 of *The Taming of the Shrew*: when Petruchio has announced that they have to leave before the wedding banquet, Lucentio and Baptista beg him to stay without success. Then Katherine tries:

> Now if you love me, stay.
> Petruchio: Grumio, my horse.

This is clearly a single line, of 10 or 11 syllables depending on how you pronounce the servant's name, and so the "rule" of verse means that it has to be continuous or the rhythm is destroyed. This is fine if it is the immediate response of a chauvinist bully, but less fine for those of us who believe he does love her, and that he is responding to her first mention of love between them. Most actors want to put the pause in the middle:

> Katherine: Now if you love me, stay.
> *(Pause as Petruchio summons up the will to hurt her publicly)*
> Petruchio: Grumio, my horse.

When I directed this with professional actors it took days of rehearsal before a moment of epiphany as to why and how we decided it worked. Yet students I have worked with have come up with a myriad of ideas, some more plausible than others, but all valid.

If mid-line endings and half lines throw up questions, so does something as small as a syllable demand respect. Most Shakespeare students know that the most famous line in world theatre is not a pentameter but an 11-syllable line. "To be or not to be, that is the question." As a consequence, the feminine ending illustrates Hamlet's girlish weakness. I am not a believer in the idea that Shakespeare thinks women are weak—quite the reverse—so I have a problem with the feminine ending theory and ask them to keep it simpler. If you just remove the extra syllable, you have a perfect revenge hero line: "To be or not to be, that is the quest." As their teacher, I love the looks and gasps of excitement when they realize that Hamlet cannot say that. Their reaction to his having to turn his "quest" into a question is always enormously gratifying.

Similarly in *Twelfth Night*, act 1 scene 5, when Olivia says to Cesario, "Your lord does know my mind, I cannot love him," the realization that the extra syllable tells you all you need to know is profound, since all through the play she's been saying that she cannot love Orsino as she has vowed seven years of mourning for her dead brother. Suddenly, faced with an eloquent, witty, and attractive young man, she launches into verse for the first time in the scene with an 11-syllable line that gives her emotions away: "I can't love Orsino, but who the hell are you?!" It's a perfect moment (in a perfect scene) of Shakespeare's using all the verbal powers he has to inform the actor: the switch into verse, the syllable count, the series of 11-syllable lines which Block describes as "open" lines rather than weak feminine endings. These all point the actor playing Olivia the way the character is going, that is, as long as the textual questions are recognized and fully explored.

One of the great joys of working on text with students is watching them realize both that it is a tool to help the actor understand the character and the play, and also that their response to it, individual and personal as it may be, is in no way less valid than that of the editor of the latest edition. I believe that this empowers students to come forward, to think proactively about what the plays mean to them, and to respond in a way that merely teaching the plays cannot achieve. If they believe that they have something to offer the texts, they tend to ask the right questions, knowing that the most obvious can be the most telling, and that the plays belong to them just as much as to those of us who make a living teaching them.

## Notes

1  *The Arden Shakespeare: Complete Works.*
2  The citations for Shakespeare are from The Arden Shakespeare: Complete Works, ed. Ann Thompson et al. (New York and London: Bloomsbury/Methuen, 2011).

# 3

# Re-entering *Macbeth*: "Witches Vanish" and Other Stage Directions

## S. P. Cerasano

When undergraduate students first engage with Shakespeare's texts they struggle to "think visually," especially with regard to stage directions. A simple "exit" or "enter" seem merely to be ways of getting an actor onto or off the stage. Encouraging students to read stage directions as something more significant is a challenge, and it is complicated in *Macbeth*, where the entrances and exits often signal kinds of "appearances" and "disappearances." The one obvious case in which this pertains occurs just after 1.3.78[1] where the text states that the three "Weird Sisters" don't "exit," but magically "vanish." This moment is fascinating in itself; however, reading other stage directions with an eye to the idea of vanishing also repays our attention, broadening the sense of the supernatural in the play, extending it to a series of characters, events, and outcomes, and raising questions concerning the fragility of human existence. Moreover, spending time with these cues enriches both our reading of the play and our understanding of the play in performance. How do the witches "vanish"? How does the "vanishing" define the nature of these characters? Is the ghost of Banquo frightening because it enters ("appears") as an insubstantial entity, or because it is "half substantial," existing in a dimension that connects the living and the dead? When students "enter" a play in which otherworldly creatures "vanish," the dead reappear, a dagger is imagined hanging in the air, and numerous characters "vanish" permanently in death, stage directions become more evocative than they initially comprehend—and nowhere more so than in *Macbeth*, where "vanishing" creates a dynamic texture within the play.

Experience has taught me that students understand very little about stage action. The subtler elements of stage traffic elude them. The symbolic aspects that a gesture can carry mystify them. They don't understand that a specific action might create a layered sense of meaning or that a single gesture can grow into something more telling, beyond the immediate moment, even gathering significance as a production unfolds and eventually turning into a "visual quotation." As a result, I start teaching with some close reading exercises. Students need to move from the simple "enter" to envisioning how a character such as Macbeth will walk, stand, or leave the stage. In the beginning it is useful to ask them to define their preconceptions. Keeping the questions simple, I focus on a few examples that employ the simple direction "enter." For instance, how will Macbeth's entrance at 1.4.14, where he arrives straight from the battlefield, differ from that at 2.2.9, in which he enters alone and speaks with Lady Macbeth just before they execute the last steps of their fiendish plan? Having articulated these differences, I then ask the students how they know that two or more instances of "enter"-ing can differ markedly when the classroom text only specifies basic cues. I return to the printed page, where students are surprised to learn that what seemed so clear in terms of the way they visualized a performance was actually an amalgamation of the text and their imagination. Of course, Macbeth's bearing on the battlefield would differ markedly from his entrance under cover of night, moments before he is about to murder Duncan. A comparison of the students' assumptions with the streamlined rhetoric of stage directions leads them ultimately to the understanding that a printed stage direction only serves as an initial step in guiding performance.

Concluding this first section, I take the opportunity to lead students through some basics about stage directions.

I have them return to 2.2 to see how stage movement is suggested by both printed cues and context. In the course of this conversation students come to understand how stage action supports and energizes the verse; how, as Macbeth and his wife move closer together and further apart, the movement choreographs the conversation. I move on and select some examples of other stage cues from different places in the play, because this conversation also presents an opportunity to show students examples of the text from old and new editions, including the First Folio (F1623), modern student texts, and even the rather scandalous "No Fear Shakespeare" in which, throughout the text, the original "Enter a servant" has been consistently altered to "A servant enters." During this part of the lesson students learn the fundamentals of movement within a play. These are: that a stage direction is essentially a cue that *begins* an action (or a set of actions); that "enter," in a printed source, occurs just before a character begins to speak; that even in early performances, dramatists were cognizant of the spaces in which a play would be performed and therefore they allowed time in their script for the actors to "enter"; and, lastly, that "exeunt" ("they exit") allows the actors to leave the space individually, together or in small groups, and even in different directions, as opposed to moving offstage together as a herd.

It was in working through *Macbeth* with students that I first came to realize that the exits are unusually redolent. In fact, one prompt, associated primarily with the "Weird Sisters" and occurring just after 1.3.78, is astonishingly evocative. It consists of only two words: "Witches vanish." Perhaps it goes without saying that actors are material beings and that disappearing is rarely in their consciousness. Yet despite the intense interest that mystery held for early modern dramatists, "vanishing" was seldom utilized, and probably for good reason. The cue to "vanish" calls for spectacle, which is more much complex to create than straightforward action, and if overdone, spectacle ceases to surprise. Besides, "vanish"-ing was associated with witches, ghosts, and apparitions—kinds of characters that have arresting, although limited, appeal. Therefore, although the cue is rare, few will be surprised to learn that, in all of Shakespeare's plays, the "vanish"-ing prompt is found most frequently in *Macbeth*, where it guides stage action, helps to define the supernatural characters, and demonstrates the power of the supernatural.[2]

I use class discussion, among other things, to explore stage cues and original sources. As it turns out, the idea of "vanishing" witches wasn't a product of Shakespeare's imagination, nor did it begin when Shakespeare consulted his best-known source, Raphael Holinshed's *The Chronicles of England, Scotlande, and Ireland*, 2 vols. (1577). Rather, it was taken from an earlier narrative, Hector Boece's *Scotum Historiae* (1527, 1540), in which the author writes that after Macbeth and Banquo interacted with the witches the "Weird Sisters" disappeared. In Boece's Scottish dialect: "As sone as thie wourdis wer said, thay suddanlie euanist out of sycht" ("As soon as their words were said, they suddenly vanished out of sight," 12th book, Fol. C. lxxiii). Consequently, Holinshed merely repeats the detail: "Herewith the foresaid women vanished immediatlie out of their sight" (vol. 2, p. 243).

After students have seen that "vanishing" was derived from Shakespeare's sources it is time to explore its manifestation in the play. One way to go about this is to produce a list of ways in which the First Folio (F1623) and some subsequent editors have handled the stage direction for "vanishing." (I inform the class that the Hecate scenes [3.5 and 4.1] are now thought to have been additions to the play contributed by another dramatist. Despite this, I include prompts from these scenes in the discussion of "vanishing.") Students quickly discover that in F1623, following 1.3.78, the prompt simply states "Witches vanish," which becomes the conventional stage direction in modern editions. Moving to a much later scene, I point out that there is another place in which "vanish" is expressly used. At 4.1.131, after the appearances of apparitions and the promenade of kings, is this cue, taken from the most recent Arden edition: *"Music. The Witches dance and vanish."* Again, a comparison of texts suggests that most editors agree to adopt this stage direction. For the moment, my students think that they have sorted out the entire puzzle. After all, they comprehend that "vanish" indicates an exit associated with supernatural characters, and if modern editors "agree" on how to signify stage directions can there really be more to say about the act of "vanishing"? Yet if I push the students to look more closely, they begin to detect some ways that aspects of "vanishing" can inspire further insights.

For one thing, they need to think through the pragmatics of "vanishing" in performance. I start by bringing them into contact with something utterly familiar—a cartoon retelling of *Macbeth*, specifically the graphic novel version of *Macbeth* first published in 2008 (Birmingham, UK: Classical Comics Ltd) with original artwork by Jon Howard. On page 15 in the top frame, the third witch states, "So all hail, Macbeth and Banquo!" her left arm pointing forward, as if to indict Macbeth. Puffs of smoke surround the figures as the witches prepare to make their exit. In the second frame down, the three witches are depicted as a pack of horrifying creatures, their eyes colored bright red so that they stand out eerily from their black habits and faces. Macbeth fearfully stands at a distance, on the left side of the frame. He points his left index finger at the witches, perhaps in an attempt to stave off whatever dark energy might be flowing in his direction. In this frame vapors engulf the witches, a mist that allows them to "vanish" from the page. In the next frame they have disappeared altogether from view. The disappearance is reinforced by the confusion in the subsequent conversation between Banquo and Macbeth. Banquo asks, "Wither are they vanished?" Macbeth responds, "Into the air, and what seem'd corporal, / Melted, as breath into the wind." In this medium it is easy to convey the disappearance of the witches.

It is a short leap from this discussion to film representations of the same action. I use two versions, one new and the other somewhat older. The first is Roman Polanski's 1971 version of *Macbeth*, in which the audience is introduced to the witches, who are coarse, unattractive women of different ages. In the opening moments of the film, the sisters are burying various objects on a rocky beach. Having completed their task they walk away from the camera, slowly disappearing into thick mist that blows in from the sea. Opening credits follow, which disappear into the same mist. Then Macbeth and Banquo spy the witches. They follow them to their hovel and enter into conversation, after which the Weird Sisters disappear down a set of steps into a subterranean lair, slamming the door shut in the men's faces. Polanski doesn't create a physical "vanishing" in the sense that we might envision it. The witches simply put an end to the interaction. Polanski's choices prompt students to confront not only the many senses of a word like "vanish," but the effects of the director's decision. What does the slamming door symbolize in terms of the immediate interaction? Does shutting the door, as a device to stop the conversation, resonate elsewhere in the film? What are the other "closed doors" that Macbeth runs up against? Who really controls the interactions between Macbeth and the witches?

The second film I use is the Michael Fassbender version (2015). During the opening scene we witness the funeral of a child while the parents, Macbeth and Lady Macbeth, look on. They are surrounded by supporters in black cloaks. All the women wear headscarves and are indistinguishable from one another. The witches, rough-hewn women dressed identically to the mourners, stand at a distance; they recite only the "Fair is foul" portion of their lines in 1.1. At the end of the ceremony the witches emerge from a mist-covered field. Having concluded their prophecy, the witches simply drift back into the fields amidst the mist. The treatment is similar later, at the beginning of 4.1, when Macbeth returns to consult with the witches; in order to convey the act of "vanishing," Fassbender uses the simplest possible technique.

When discussing how to stage "vanishing" it helps if students visualize the elements of the familiar large public playhouses that early modern actors would have had at their disposal, such as the Globe. Illustrations of the early playhouses, or of the current Globe in London, all assist students in imagining the dimensions of the larger public theatres and the various architectural features that actors and dramatists had at their disposal. The eminent theatre architect C. Walter Hodges posited that four or more trap doors would have provided a variety of portals for entrances and exits. Some of the traps were probably equipped with winches that raised and lowered platforms on which objects, such as cauldrons, could have rested. If the trap was large enough, the witches could have ridden up onto the stage along with the cauldron. In Hodges' view other traps were probably fitted out with stairs or ladders so that a group of characters could have entered from below the stage together, or in a line, as in the procession of kings in 4.1.

The larger openings in the stage floor had other purposes as well. The smoke that ordinarily surrounded supernatural figures might have been generated from chunks of smoldering peat placed under and within the cauldron.[3] Not only this, but smoke could have been made using coal in chafers under the stage. Various substances could easily have been scattered over the coals to generate smoke that wafted up through the openings around the traps, producing a "smoke screen" for the actual space through which the actors passed. And there is one more possibility: the actors could have hidden the "vanishing" by using strategically placed furniture on the stage. A banquet table, covered by a long table cloth extending to the floor, offered a screen for the trap areas located behind it. Banquo's ghost probably came up through a trap located behind a table when he appeared at the banquet, unnerving Macbeth and punning on his own name (3.4.35).

All of this discussion, centered on the physical attributes of the public playhouse, renders a sense of how the vanishing would have *looked*. Yet the staging was more complex than simply putting up a smoke screen or disappearing down into the bowels of the playhouse beneath the stage. Students are able to identify with the full mechanics of the stage action when they realize that "vanishing" was very similar to performing a magic trick where the spectators are deceived largely through a series of distractions. Most importantly, there were two aural diversions: thunder and music. From the beginning, thunder accompanies the entrances and exits of the witches. In practice, thunder might have come from multiple points around the playhouse, from underneath and behind the stage. (Lightning was created through the use of firecrackers.) Alternately, loud and cacophonous music (see 4.1.131) interrupts the audience's attention while "The Witches Dance, and vanish."

It's clear that *Macbeth* was performed at a large public theatre—and specifically the Globe—in 1611 when the astrologer Simon Forman saw the play;[4] however, the times and venues of other possible performances, including any initial performances done earlier in the century, are unknown. Nevertheless, one further question can be explored hypothetically: what factors bearing upon the matter of "vanishing" would have been different if the play had been performed at a smaller, private theatre, such as the Blackfriars, which was also owned by Shakespeare and his company? Of course, both public and private playhouses would have shared some basic features. Most importantly, a number of trap doors would have allowed movement into the under-area of the stage in the Blackfriars. But the effect created by the modest size of the Blackfriars space and the closeness of the audience to the stage are likewise open to consideration. Students can expand their investigation even further if they envisage the marked change of environment that would have been created by performing a play like *Macbeth* within a roofed space in which actors played at night with only torches and candles for lighting. Such performance conditions would have highlighted the supernatural atmosphere of *Macbeth* and intensified the sense of various characters' "vanishing." Certainly the darkness alone would have assisted the actors in simulating a sense of melting into blackness, probably lessening the amount of smoke and other kinds of masking devices that would have been necessary on the large public stages where plays were performed during the afternoon and in full daylight. Not least of all, as modern spectators who have experienced horror films like the *Halloween* series, students can easily imagine the fear and claustrophobia—to say nothing of the mounting anxiety—that certain scenes of *Macbeth* would have provoked within the close, shadowy space that could easily have been fabricated within the Blackfriars.

At this point it is useful to survey some historical and cultural contexts. Students are interested to learn that, for Shakespeare's audience, the sense of vanishing went together naturally with the capabilities ascribed to witches by many persons in early modern England. Well-known writers (including the highly skeptical Reginald Scot, whose *Discovery of Witchcraft* [1584] Shakespeare had read) reported that a number of their contemporaries believed that witches were able to do things "beyond human nature." For example, the anonymous writer of *News from Scotland* (1591–1592?) commented that witches were absolutely capable of sailing in sieves, which Shakespeare references early in the play: "But in a sieve I'll thither sail, / And like a rat without a tail, / I'll do, I'll do, I'll do" (1.3.8–10). Additionally, witches were believed to create thunder and lightning and to raise tempests. So "vanishing" was one of their signature feats and it was an action that destabilized its human observers. Creatures that "vanish"-ed were otherworldly, explaining Banquo's initial description of them as "So withered and so wild in their attire, / That look not like th'inhabitants o'th'earth, / And yet are on't" (1.3.40–42).

Having arrived at this place, I shift attention a bit to Shakespeare's use of other "insubstantial" objects in the play. Curiously, the dagger conjured by Macbeth's mind at 2.1.33–34 ("Is this a dagger which I see before me, / The handle toward my hand?") occasionally appears and disappears in film interpretations, but it doesn't actually "enter" or "exit." Macbeth can't quite decide on the exact nature of the dagger; whether the vision is "but / A dagger of the mind, a false creation" (38). In contrast, the ghost of Banquo "exits" and "enters," referred to by Macbeth as a "horrible shadow" (3.4.106). When Banquo's phantom follows the show of kings he seems to "vanish" along with the others, but upon his first entrance Banquo is substantial enough to "*sit* in Macbeth's place" (3.4.35 s.d., emphasis mine). The intriguing point is that the actor is corporal while the ghost is incorporeal. I ask my students whether perhaps it's the "half corporeality" that helps to create the horror of the witches vanishing and the ghost sitting.

Likewise, the apparitions in 4.1 vanish; however, the action is encoded into the text differently. All of them arrive following a clap of thunder; all "descend" when they leave the stage. (Owing to their previous analysis, students should realize that "descends" indicates a movement down under the stage through one of the traps and is an alternative for "vanishes.") In the same scene the witches are introduced similarly by a clap of thunder. Later on, accompanied by music, they also presumably descend; a stage direction states "The Witches dance, and vanish" (131 s.d.). So the apparitions "vanish," like the witches, accompanied by noise and a smoke screen. The F1623 text doesn't specify how the procession of kings, followed by the ghost of Banquo, leave the stage. Most editors emend the text by adding "Exeunt kings and Banquo" (123 s.d.). Although "Exeunt" is the most conservative option if the kings exit as the other apparitions, "descend"-ing down one or more traps and "vanish"-ing.

Given the irony and dark humor in *Macbeth*, students can easily consider the metaphorical uses of "vanishing," particularly because so many characters "vanish permanently" in the course of the play. The Weird Sisters "vanish" forever after four scenes (if we accept all of the material in 1.1, 1.3, 3.5, and 4.1 as belonging to the play). To these we can add Banquo and King Duncan, Lady Macduff, her son, and Lady Macbeth (who seems to have borne children, dead before the opening of the play). The two murderers who are sent to kill Banquo and Fleance, although sent out again to dispatch Macduff's family (4.2), are potentially put to death as well. (In Polanski's film they are shown a door down a set of dark steps into a dungeon and their own deaths.) There is the death of the traitorous Thane of Cawdor at the opening of the play (noted in the text and visualized brutally in Polanski's film). Enlarging the numbers are the apparitions of the dead kings. Not only this, but the play ends with Macbeth's own death, vividly displayed in his decapitated image: "*Enter* Macduff *with Macbeth's head*" (5.9.19 s.d.).

This lengthy list makes the point that "vanishing" through death pervades the play, but there is one additional group of "vanishings"—characters who appear only once— that I ask students to identify. Here, students discover four more "vanishings": the Porter (2.3), the Old Man (2.4), a waiting-gentlewoman (5.1), and Young Siward (5.7). A few other characters, in related fashion, are fleeting and, as such, they enlarge the sense of disappearance in the play. Hecate appears in two different places (3.5 and 4.1), as do Menteith and Caithness (5.2, 5.4) and Seyton (5.3, 5.5). A few other characters appear briefly, including the doctor and a messenger (4.3, 5.1, 5.3 and 1.5, 4.2, 5.5). Fleance "flees," never to return. Malcolm and Donalbain flee following the king's death (2.4.25–26) and Donalbain disappears from sight. As the play moves to its conclusion, Caithness asks, "Who knows if Donalbain be with his brother?" To which Lennox answers, "For certain, sir, he is not" (5.2.7–8). During the final minutes of the Polanski film, Donalbain is provocatively shown traveling back to the witches' hovel; another nightmare is in the making. Nevertheless, if we follow the text, Donalbain potentially becomes just another "vanishing" character.

## Notes

1 All textual references are to the Arden edition of *Macbeth*, edited by Sandra Clark and Pamela Mason (London and New York: Bloomsbury, 2015).
2 The other notable inclusion of vanishing occurs in *The Tempest*, 3.3.52 s.d., when a banquet disappears from in front of the hungry lords Alonso, Sebastian, and Gonzalo: "*Thunder and lightning. Enter Ariel, like a harpy; claps his wings upon the table; and with a quaint device the banquet vanishes.*" Quoted from *The Tempest*, ed. Virginia Mason Vaughan and Alden T. Vaughan (London and New York: Bloomsbury, 2011). Later, in the same scene following line 82, there is the direction: "*He* [Ariel] *vanishes in thunder.*"
3 C. Walter Hodges, *Enter the Whole Army* (Cambridge: Cambridge University Press, 1999), 123.

4 Forman's notes are recorded in his *Booke of Plaies* (Bodleian
Library, MS. Ashmole 208, fols. 207r–v), transcribed in E. K.
Chambers, *William Shakespeare: A Study of Facts and Problems*,
2 vols. (Oxford: Clarendon Press, 1930), 2: 337–338 (slightly
modernized) and A. L. Rowse, *Simon Forman: Sex and Society
in Shakespeare's Age* (London: Weidenfeld and Nicolson, 1974),
303–304 (completely modernized).

# 4

# Seeing the Elizabethan Playhouse in *Richard II*

## *Joseph Candido*

At the first meeting of my undergraduate Shakespeare class each semester I perform an academic ritual that is, I suspect, drearily familiar to most teachers and students: I hand out the syllabus for the course, along with an illustration of a typical Elizabethan playhouse. The syllabus is, of course, new to the students, but the illustration of the playhouse is old hat for many—indeed, some have even built a model of the structure in their high school English class for extra credit. They know all about Shakespeare's stage. But after dutifully rehearsing in my opening lecture the familiar facts about the Elizabethan outdoor theatre—the trap door, the heavens, the discovery space, the tiring house, the upper stage, etc.—I dismay my students a bit further with our first assignment. Not only are they to have *Richard II* read entirely for the next meeting, they must also be ready to identify at least one episode or moment in the play where our response to the action is enriched by our understanding of how the scene might have looked on Shakespeare's stage, a task they hardly seem to relish. Nevertheless, our second meeting always brings happy surprises. I never fail to be impressed by the number of students who, fresh from a near-mortal battle with blank verse, rhyming couplets, and characters with confusing family names, enter wholeheartedly into a discussion of the assignment. I must admit that, even for an old-fashioned lecturer like myself, this

second day of class remains one of my favorites, for in it I get
the pleasure of seeing students beginning to change their idea
of the Elizabethan theatre from one of a dead and ancient
"model" to that of a dynamically expressive space inhabited
by real people acting out critical events in their lives. This
change of perspective greatly enriches our discussions for the
remainder of the semester, particularly during those moments
when we pause from our treatment of language and theme to
consider how seeing events in the playing space for which they
were written gives us another "language," a visual language,
that, existing hand-in-hand with Shakespeare's spoken words,
creates deeply meaningful stage pictures.

A fine example of this visual language occurs in an episode that makes the students' list less frequently than others,
but one that does get cited from time to time by the most per-
ceptive members of the class: the brief conversation between
York and Bolingbroke at 3.3.15–17.[1] The scene opens with
disarming simplicity. York, Bolingbroke, Northumberland,
and other followers of the Duke gather on the grounds before
Flint Castle to discuss military matters. Northumberland,
ever insensitive to verbal niceties, refers hastily to the
king as "Richard" and is rebuked for doing so by York.
Northumberland's weak defense of his disrespectfulness, "…
only to be brief / Left I his title out" (3.3.10–11), gives rise to
the following dialogue:

York                              The time hath been,
       Would you have been so brief with him, he would
       Have been so brief with you to shorten you,
       For taking so the head, your whole head's length.
Bol.   Mistake not, uncle, further than you should.
York   Take not, good cousin, further than you should,
       Lest you mis-take: the heavens are o'er our heads.
                                        (3.3.11–17)

Most students grasp after a few moments of prodding that
this brief interchange must occur in the very center of the
stage, directly under "the heavens" to which York so explicitly alludes, with their clearly visible representations of the

sun, moon, stars, and signs of the zodiac. All well and good. Now most of the class can see that York, by his simple gesture toward the canopy above, is making it perfectly clear to Bolingbroke that God is watching everything they do and that careless statements like Northumberland's as well as crassly ambitious intentions like Bolingbroke's occur in an ever-present religious context where the deposing of a king has divine as well as earthly significance. The heavens—and by analogy God—are as unchanging and ever-present as the canopy, which remains firmly in place and unavoidably visible throughout the play, hovering over each and every action of *Richard II*. This is, of course, the very idea that Richard affirms so repeatedly throughout the play, most noticeably in his magnificent aria upon returning to England from Ireland (3.2.36ff.), with its fanciful and extended allusion to the sun, "the searching eye of heaven" (clearly visible under the canopy), rising in the east to expose the "sin" of Bolingbroke (37, 53).

But the conversation between York and Bolingbroke has an additional layer of complexity that even good students sometimes fail to see. I ask the class to look again at their representation of the Elizabethan outdoor theatre. Is there anything else on the stage that invests the scene with even further significance? Almost immediately they recognize the point. Directly under the feet of Bolingbroke and York is the equally omnipresent trap door, the object that in the vocabulary of the Elizabethan stage represents the entryway to hell. It is a pleasure for me to see how the scene begins to enlarge in the imagination of my students once they understand that the actions of Bolingbroke and York, like those of all other characters in the play, are literally played out in the space between two powerfully opposite (and visible) moral extremes: heaven and hell. Richard's repeated allusions to God, heavenly angels, Divine Right, and the like may now seem far less fanciful and self-deluded to them than they seemed at first blush. His vocabulary, quite literally, is that of the Elizabethan stage. With this observation in mind, we can rediscover the character as not merely a poetic dreamer with a frail grasp on reality, but as a character who engages directly with essentially real—indeed, visually concrete—features of his world. Moreover, we come back to the significance of the space under the canopy time and time again for the remainder of the semester. Newly aware of the possible symbolism of a character simply standing in a particular place on the stage, students can bring a whole new dimension to their understanding of characters like Henry V, Hamlet, Macbeth, Angelo, and many others. One of my favorite questions in class, and one that students often anticipate, is "Where might this scene be played"? The prayer scene in *Hamlet*, Prince John's treachery in *2 Henry IV*, Angelo's attempt to deflower Isabella, the great trial scenes in *Measure for Measure* and *The Merchant of Venice*, the deposition scene in *Richard II*: these are all episodes that we discuss as acquiring a much richer level of irony if played in the space directly under the canopy and above the trap door. It is one thing to tell students at the beginning of class that every action in Shakespeare's world is fraught with serious moral and religious consequences, but it is quite another when students are able to see, so to speak, the Elizabethan stage making the same point.

A fascinating stage moment that seems to encapsulate the play's central concern with the pattern of rising and falling, and an episode that never fails to be noticed by students as a good example of the uses to which Shakespeare puts the resources of his stage, comes very shortly after the York–Bolingbroke conversation: it is Richard's dramatic descent from the walls of Flint Castle to encounter Bolingbroke in the base court below (3.3.178–186):

North.      My lord, in the base court he [i.e., Bolingbroke]
              doth attend
            To speak with you. May it please you to come
            down?
K. Richard  Down, down I come, like glist'ring Phaëton,
            Wanting the manage of unruly jades.
            In the base court? Base court where kings grow
            base
            To come at traitors' calls and do them grace.

> In the base court? Come down? Down court,
> down king!
> For night-owls shriek where mounting larks
> should sing. [*Exeunt King Richard and his
> Followers from above.*]
> [*Northumberland returns to Bolingbroke.*]
>
> (3.3.176–183)

Since we have already briefly discussed in class the *de
casibus* theme and its relation to the rise-and-fall structure
of the play, this scene is a relatively easy one for students
to identify as an example of Shakespeare's use of the two
different playing levels of the stage in order to underscore
symbolic action. But again, as in the York–Bolingbroke
episode, there is far more here than meets the eye. I like
to begin the consideration of this episode with two simple
questions for the students: 1) how might Richard get down
from the upper stage to the main playing area, and 2) when
does the action begin and how long might it take? I mention
to the class that the authoritative text for *Richard II* (the
Quarto of 1597) includes no stage directions for the episode,
so we needn't in this instance be completely influenced by
the interpolated stage directions of later editors, who always
have Richard exiting from above *after* his speech at line 183.
I re-read the passage aloud two or three times in class and
ask students to ignore the stage direction. Rather, I want
them to decide for themselves when it would be most prob-
able for Richard to begin his descent. There are, of course,
disagreements, but a substantial number of the class
(perhaps because I've invited them to question scholarly
authority) say that it would be more natural for Richard to
begin his descent at the words "Down, down I come." After
all, who indicates that he is in the act of coming down when
in fact he is standing still? In order to leaven the discussion, I like to remind students at this juncture that on at
least two occasions earlier in the play Richard has called
specific attention to his strange attraction to downward
motion, and on both of them he appears to be enacting his
words as he speaks them. The first occurs just before the

aborted joust between Bolingbroke and Mowbray when the king proclaims, "We will descend and fold him [Bolingbroke] in our arms" (1.3.54), and the second, far more analogous to the scene we are discussing, occurs after Richard's return from Ireland when he begins to grasp the hopelessness of his cause: "For God's sake let us sit upon the ground / And tell sad stories of the death of kings—" (3.2.155–156). Clearly, Richard has a penchant at times for describing his actions while in the very process of enacting them, particularly those that involve downward movement.

"OK," I say, now let's suppose that Richard begins his descent at 3.3.178. How does he get down? It doesn't take long for the class to determine that there must be some sort of staircase or ladder behind the tiring house for this purpose, since obviously a ladder positioned on the outside of the castle walls would be both dramatically and technically untenable. In short order we begin to discuss the obvious: that is, that for a very considerable period of stage time—especially if Richard starts to come down at line 178, but even if he starts his descent at line 183—he literally disappears from view. Again, the mere physical configuration of the Elizabethan stage allows Shakespeare the opportunity to make a stunning (and for contemporary audiences a terrifying) point: the audience in the theatre is forced to contemplate, for however long or short a period of time, a world with a vanishing king. As in the York–Bolingbroke episode, the stage picture here reflects much of the linguistic texture of the play. It gives us, for example, a remarkably apt visual rendering of the disappearing monarch who, during the deposition scene, wishes that he "were a mockery king of snow, / Standing before the sun of Bolingbroke, / To melt myself away in water drops!" (4.1.260–262), and is completely in line with the lonely, imprisoned figure at the end of the play who affirms "But whate'er I be, / Nor I nor any man that but man is / With nothing shall be pleased, till he be eased / With being nothing" (5.5.38–41). As Richard descends from the upper level of the stage and vanishes behind the tiring house, Shakespeare once more uses the resources of his theatre to re-create pictorially Richard's chief anxiety—and later, ironically, his deep longing—of vanishing from view.

But there is still one more point in the episode for us to discuss; namely, does it matter how long Richard remains unseen? Let's assume that Richard does indeed begin his descent at line 183 and appears on the main stage, as all modern editors would have it, a mere two lines later at line 185. In this scenario the king still remains unseen for a period of time, however brief, and the audience is still able to contemplate (some scholars would say anticipate with dread) the prospect of a fractured society with an absent and soon-to-be-deposed king. But I like to push the argument just a bit further here. I invite the students to consider what the likelihood is that in the short space of time occupied by two spoken lines we could expect the actor playing Richard to appear on the main stage below in a stately fashion. Perhaps, as many editors suggest, there occurs some sort of flourish to occupy the dead time between Richard's descent and his appearance among Bolingbroke and his followers at line 185. Charles R. Forker's interpolated stage direction in his 2002 Arden edition of the play is typical of the practice of many modern editors: "[*Flourish. Enter below* KING RICHARD *and his Followers*]." What I now like to ask students in light of this possibility is exactly what sort of theatrical decision they would make if they were staging the scene and, moreover, what possible thematic implications might be suggested by their decision. A flourish at line 185 would certainly alleviate the temporal problem and fill the theatre with a musical sequence entirely familiar to spectators at an Elizabethan outdoor playhouse. But what if just the opposite occurs? What if Richard does in fact begin his descent at line 178, and instead of the flourish accompanying a royal entry, we hear instead the muffled, fading, hidden voice of a disappearing king, sounds that few spectators at the theatre could possibly anticipate at this juncture? Bolingbroke's question to Northumberland, "What says his majesty?" (184), could in this context be understood as indicating that he and the rest of his followers (excepting Northumberland, who is closest to the king) cannot quite decipher what Richard is saying. With this possibility in mind, I like to remind my students that Shakespeare frequently makes use of off-stage utterances (for example, voices "within"), as well as other more extended stage moments when characters, although invisible to the audience, nonetheless speak for an extended period of time. The Ghost in *Hamlet* giving orders from underneath the stage and Malvolio in *Twelfth Night* in his "dark room" (probably in "hell" under the trap door) come immediately to mind. A further point I try to make here is that in this instance from *Richard II* we might also be encountering a moment of uneasy silence on the lower stage as Richard makes his slow, barely audible descent to the place where Bolingbroke awaits. The whole awkward scene would be characterized by silence, slowness, and some degree of inaudibility. We all agree that it is highly improbable that Richard would be in a hurry to descend; rather he would be far more likely here, as he does in the deposition scene, to create moments of prolonged or embarrassing silence. I always ask my students at this point what effect silence creates in the theatre when we are waiting for language. They have all read *Waiting for Godot*, and I find the allusion to Beckett at this point to work as a real eye-opener for some students. I then make a further analogy to a situation much closer to home—the silence that descends on a classroom when a teacher poses a question that no one wants to answer. What is that period of silence like? It may only last a few seconds, but it seems much longer. I invite the students to imagine that in the scene from *Richard II* something very like that unsettling moment might occur. Once we entertain that possibility, a dramatic action that seems completely straightforward suddenly opens up to us to reveal a whole new range of critical possibilities.

I should say in all candor that my intention in raising the above questions with students is decidedly *not* to attempt to dismantle a long-held editorial tradition or to establish a "correct" way of playing the scene on an Elizabethan stage. Indeed, if I were editing *Richard II*, I would be strongly tempted to follow my scholarly predecessors in placing the stage direction indicating Richard's exit from above precisely where it usually appears—at the end of line 183. The idea of a long flourish, combined with Northumberland's two-line response to Bolingbroke's question ("Sorrow and grief of heart / Makes him speak fondly like a frantic man. / Yet he is come" (184–186), would no doubt provide sufficient time for Richard to make an appropriately royal appearance, especially if Northumberland and Bolingbroke engage in some sort of relevant stage business while they wait for Richard's arrival. It would also allow for the splendid lines Richard speaks to be fully heard and absorbed by the audience. The purpose of my little in-class exercise is in no way to assail our editorial forbears or even to encourage students to do so (at least not without good cause). Nor do I intend to suggest that there is a "right" or "wrong" way to play the scene. Rather, the sole aim of the exercise is to get students to think creatively about the myriad symbolic and thematic possibilities that the mere physical aspects of an Elizabethan theatre provide for them. I want students to try to approach each dramatic action in a Shakespearean play, no matter how small, as an opportunity to engage with the Elizabethan playhouse as an interpretive space that opens up thematic vistas to them rather than one which closes them out.

Moreover, such thematic vistas can come upon us in surprising, often indirect, ways. For example, when we as teachers remind students of the basic characteristics of the Elizabethan stage, we always emphasize that the theatre has very little in the way of scenery. Our usual follow-up to this observation is that as a result we as readers must pay close attention to the text in order to reconstruct as best we can in our imaginations just what the physical surroundings of any scene might be or how actors are behaving. Or, in the words of the Chorus in *Henry V*, we must "piece out [the theatre's] imperfections with [our] thoughts" (Chorus 1, 23). Seldom, if ever, do we think of the absence of scenery on Shakespeare's stage as a good thing, but I would like to submit that there is one brief moment in *The Tempest* when the very "imperfections" of the stage—in this case its almost complete lack of scenery—actually help us to come to a clearer understanding of the characters speaking as well as a wide range of thematic matters. The scene occurs in 2.1 as Alonso, Sebastian, Antonio, Adrian, and Gonzalo are discussing the nature of the place in which they find themselves. I love to go over one small moment in this scene in order to ask my students exactly what the island of *The Tempest* looks like:

Gon.  Here is every thing advantageous to life.
Ant.  True, save means to live.
Seb.  Of that there's none, or little.
Gon.  How lush and lusty the grass looks! How green!
Ant.  The ground indeed is tawny.
Seb.  With an eye of green in't.
Ant.  He misses not much.
Seb.  No; he doth but mistake the truth totally.

(2.1.50–57)

Is the island green or tawny? The playhouse refuses to speak to us on this matter and, I tell my students, that is precisely the point. The very absence of scenery here puts the onus on us to decide which of these various speakers we trust to describe the true properties of the island, and further, how we as audience members see the island in our own dramatic imaginations. I like to remind students that one of the great recurring themes of Shakespeare's plays, and one that we have been tracing throughout the semester by the time we read *The Tempest*, is the power of the human imagination to create reality. Gonzalo sees one thing; Antonio and Sebastian see another. What do we see? In appealing to our creative imagination at this point in the play Shakespeare forces us, simply by exploiting one of the "deficiencies" of his stage, to decide how we might feel about a whole range of issues embodied in the two contrary ways of seeing the island— that is, the nature of the New World, the extent to which we can regard it as "Edenesque," our capability to recover lost innocence, the stubbornness of evil in a world striving for personal and societal renewal, etc.

In one way or another we are always involved in a direct encounter with the stage in Shakespeare's plays, either piecing out its imperfections or being stimulated by its imaginative possibilities. The great Globe itself makes very sure of that.

## Note

1 All citations of *Richard II* are from the Arden edition of Charles R. Forker (London: Thomson Learning, 2002). All other references to Shakespeare are to the *The Riverside Shakespeare*, ed. G. Blakemore Evans et al. (Boston: Houghton Mifflin, 1974). I have silently regularized the speech headings for both editions.

# SECTION TWO

## Learning through Performance

# SECTION TWO

## Learning through Performance

# 5

# Acting as Ownership in the Shakespeare Classroom

## James C. Bulman and Beth Watkins

We began with a problem. How could we, as veteran teachers of acting, directing, and drama of all periods, devise a team-taught course that might more successfully lead students to take ownership of Shakespeare? Jim (English) for years had taught a Shakespeare survey course in which viewing performance figured prominently. Close reading of the text was followed by analysis of film versions of each play and, when possible, theatrical performances, with the goal of encouraging students to understand a range of meanings enabled by the choices made by actors, directors, designers, and technicians. For nearly as long, Beth (Theatre) had taught acting and directing courses in which performance was understood very differently: students would learn how their own physical embodiment of a character and their own exploration of language as performative could allow them to make the leap from regarding a play as a fixed artifact to one that is dynamic, contingent, and deeply personal. What impact, we wondered, might the introduction of actor training have on students learning how to read Shakespeare?

Classroom performances, of course, have been a staple of Shakespeare courses for several decades. Teachers regularly ask students to get on their feet, rehearse in groups, and perform scenes for the class as a way of engaging them more directly with Shakespeare's language and teaching them to become active makers of meaning rather than passive observers of others' performances. By getting on their feet, it has been argued, students explore aspects of their own identities and come to a self-realization that helps to persuade them that Shakespeare is indeed their contemporary.[1] Much as they may enjoy such amateur exercises, however, students typically emerge with little understanding of how actors approach a Shakespeare text, of how much may be learned when actors are trained in the art of physically embodying a character and taught, through extended rehearsal periods, to explore the nuances of performative speech and gesture.

Our goal in devising a new course in the spring of 2017 was to merge the disciplines of literary study and actor training in a way that might convince students—many of them English majors—of the benefits of treating Shakespeare's plays as theatrical scripts. We decided to approach each play traditionally at first, instructing students on how to identify plot structure, analyze character and motivation, unpack figurative language as a means to create character, and recognize textual cues for performance. We would also discuss the traditions of genre criticism, conventions of the Elizabethan stage, historical sources and contexts, and ways in which each play may be seen to anticipate issues of current cultural significance—the abuse of political power in *Macbeth*, for instance, or the confusion of sex and gender roles in *Twelfth Night*. Such work, central to the study of Shakespeare as literature, also provided students with the tools to become good dramaturgs—tools that we expected them to use in developing scenes for performance.

We then would focus on the acquisition of acting skills: such things as vocal projection and inflection, materializing language through physical action and gesture, and working with the given circumstances of a scene to formulate a character's objectives—what the character wants— and to recognize obstacles to those objectives. It was our hope that when students learned such skills, even in a rudimentary form, their embodiment of a Shakespeare text would diminish the gulf between their twenty-first-century sensibilities and early modern texts and help them to understand the plays not as alien artifacts from a bygone age, but as living documents whose immediacy is readily apparent.

The first assignment we gave the students—to memorize and perform a sonnet of their choice—persuaded us how difficult the task we'd set for ourselves would be. Using a few well-known sonnets to illustrate the form's potential as dramatic speech ("Look in thy glass and tell the face thou viewest," "When, in disgrace with fortune and men's eyes"), we asked the students to imagine what the given circumstances of the poem might be, what objective the speaker seeks to achieve, and what obstacle stands in the way of that achievement. We talked about shifts of tone, about rhythm and meter, about the function of rhyme; as a group, we practiced using caesuras and enjambment as aids to dramatic speech. We also showed them a wonderful clip from a Royal Shakespeare Company (RSC) Master Class broadcast on ITV (*The South Bank Show*, 1979) in which Trevor Nunn explores the dramatic potentials of sonnet 138 ("When my love swears that she is made of truth") with David Suchet, who in his delivery makes clear the very things we had been discussing: given circumstances, objective and obstacle; shifts of tone and attitude; use of inflection and gesture to convey meaning. But when students performed their sonnets, they fell flat. Many of them had trouble with memorization; some seemed not to understand what they were saying; few employed the vocal variety, dynamics, and tonal shifts necessary to convince listeners of the reality of their sonnet's dramatic moment. What we learned from this exercise was that while watching an RSC actor working through a sonnet may have been instructive, students were unable to apply his methods to their own recitations. Watching did not translate into doing. Rather, they needed exercises to develop the techniques they demonstrated, and plenty of opportunity to practice them.

For the next assignment, then, we realized that we had to commit far more time to group work and acting exercises. It was evident that the students needed an introduction to a system of acting that would give them the tools to analyze dramatic action, character motivation, and situation. We also needed to help them understand that the actor's body is as important as the spoken word, so that they could connect Shakespeare's complex and often unfamiliar language with characters' physical involvement in recognizable situations. We drew on the basic Stanislavski system of emphasizing action analysis, as mentioned above: determining the given circumstances of a scene, identifying a character's objective and motivating force (how strong or weak their desire to achieve the objective), and what the major obstacle to the objective is at any given moment of the scene. While Stanislavski's system is most closely allied with contemporary psychological realism, his method of analyzing dramatic action can be applied to a wide array of theatrical and acting styles.[2] Through such action analysis of Shakespeare's text and physical exploration of character embodiment, we strove to give the students tools for tackling Shakespearean performance.

We divided the class into pairs of actors, each pair given a two-character scene of about 60 lines to memorize, rehearse, and perform for the class. The scenes were drawn from two plays that would be our focal texts for this part of the course, *Twelfth Night* and *Macbeth*, and over a three-week period we devoted most of our class time to physical and vocal work. For example, we would ask actors to stand six or eight feet from their partners and to deliver the lines they had memorized (as Lord and Lady Macbeth, or Malcolm and Macduff; as Olivia and Cesario, or Orsino and Cesario) while tossing a ball to each other on the most important action word of each line—and *only* on that word. Eventually this morphed into a more rapid exchange in which actors threw the ball as they began each line, with the expectation that it would be always in motion. In addition to forcing actors to focus on what they were saying, this ball-tossing exercise taught them to listen carefully to each other and to pick up cues without pausing between lines. Additionally, it encouraged them to experiment with tempo and rhythm and to try out diverse line readings that they hadn't previously considered.

We also asked actors to pair a gesture with each verbal image in the speech and, once that was accomplished, to enlarge that gesture. How big could it possibly be? We then asked them to create a second gesture for that same image, this one conveying more fully the emotional force of the image. Students spent the period experimenting with both gestures, varying such things as the tempo of line delivery, the height or direction of each gesture, and the position of their bodies in relation to the bodies of their acting partners. In essence, they were learning to open up and "fill" the stage, both physically and vocally, through extended gestures and dynamic line interpretations. Theatrically, these exercises gave the students permission to make stronger, bigger choices; as they did so, students came to understand that acting for the stage is not as naturalistic as for film or television, the media with which they were most familiar.

Finally, we asked the actors to consider the given circumstances of their scene as provided by the text. Who are the characters in the scene? Where does the scene take place? What previous action or backstory explains, or creates a context for, the present action? Students portraying the Macbeths, for instance, were asked to consider what is on Lady Macbeth's mind as she waits for her husband to come down from murdering King Duncan in his chamber. It is the middle of the night, and she doesn't want to be discovered awake at that hour. Nervous and excited, she is startled by an owl. Then she hears a voice. Is it her husband's or someone else's? Has their plot to murder the king been discovered? Gone awry? Has she been unnerved by watching Duncan sleeping—an image that reminded her of her father? Such considerations may seem obvious to teachers of Shakespeare, but to students they can be revelatory, in particular as they indicate the countless ways in which language—lines that are seemingly straightforward on the page—can be performative.

The emphasis on objectives and obstacles was equally new to students. Few (only those who had taken acting classes) had ever considered what their character wants and what stands in the way of achieving that objective. Being able to identify such things helped them to refine their motivation for speech and action and to consider the range of choices available to them. Viola, for example, has disguised herself as a youth to be able to find a position at Orsino's court. Our actors pondered her dilemma in trying to convince people of her male identity while finding herself attracted to the Duke she serves. To serve him honorably, she needs to persuade Olivia to allow him to be a suitor, yet emotionally, such service may work against her own desire for the Duke. How assertive should she be in her interview with Olivia? How playful? Should she, speaking in her own voice, covertly sabotage the Duke's chances as Olivia's suitor? And later, in conversation with the Duke, should she drop hints of her female identity? How dangerous to her position in his household would it be for her to reveal too much about herself—or about her interest in him? These questions helped students to understand where the conflict resided in their assigned scenes and why situations could be humorously or seriously regarded as "life or death" challenges for the character: they prompted actors to make specific and pointed, rather than generic and superficial, choices.

Having determined the given circumstances of their scenes, actors had to put the dramatic action "on its feet." Few actors had had any experience with staging, so they first needed to learn the fundamentals of blocking. Those learned, they had to figure out how their characters used tasks (or physical actions) to achieve their objectives. Olivia, for example, since she is in mourning, is at liberty to refuse to entertain all suitors. She wears a veil to obscure her face, yet it allows her to listen to what others say. When she begins to express an interest in Cesario, she agrees to his impudent request to remove her veil, an action that allows her to engage more directly and flirtatiously with him.

These acting exercises had a profound effect on the quality of the two-person scenes when they were performed for the class. Since students had studied both plays, were equally familiar with the texts, and had worked together on the various scenes during class exercises, they were prepared to share their thoughts and perspectives about how line readings and actions could or should be motivated. In the week before their scenes were performed, we asked several volunteers to present portions of their scenes for the class in a kind of open rehearsal, allowing their peers to comment, question, and suggest. It was obvious to us that they had learned a good deal about the ways in which actors approach a Shakespeare text, and these open rehearsals offered productive evidence of the actors' shared purpose and collective willingness to experiment with performance choices. Students, we realized, were experiencing first-hand how fundamentally theatre is a collaborative enterprise.

The success of using open rehearsals as a method of instruction prompted us, for a final assignment, to have all students prepare a unit from a longer scene (up to 150 lines) to present to the class two weeks prior to their final performances, allowing them sufficient time to incorporate feedback from peers into their subsequent rehearsals. We divided the class into groups of three actors, each group told to select a scene from a play we had not read in class. In other words, each group would be on its own to do dramaturgical work on its chosen play (and those choices ranged from *Two Gentlemen of Verona* to *Antony and Cleopatra*), to write a paper detailing that work, and to discover how the scene they had selected fit into that play, considering the given circumstances, objectives, and obstacles of their characters. The class was then given the opportunity to weigh in during these unit rehearsals with questions, ideas, and critiques of even the smallest details, to ensure clarity of purpose. Since many students were unfamiliar with the play from which any particular unit was taken, they formed the perfect "naive" audience in their insistence that dialogue and stage action be clear and make dramatic sense.

The class response to one such unit will illustrate the ways in which students had learned to think and behave as actors. The unit was a compressed version of the grave-digger scene in *Hamlet* (5.1), in which the two "clowns" discuss Ophelia's death just prior to the entry of Hamlet, who rather abruptly (given the cut text students used) asks them how long a man will lie in the earth ere he rot. The actors performing this unit had blocked it well, identified the clowns' malapropisms (salvation for damnation, crowner for coroner), unearthed the humor of the debate about accidental versus purposeful drowning, and made clear (even if not with full comprehension) the irony of their lines about class distinctions and privilege among "even-Christians." In a discussion with actors immediately following their rehearsal of the unit, the class made some trenchant observations. The first clown, one student observed, seems to have scholarly aspirations, to judge from his misused Latin phrases and his convoluted explanation of how an accidental drowning "shortens not" the victim's life. Why, she asked, when the clown seems to take himself so seriously, does the actor toss off these lines so lightly and play them for laughs? Further, asked another student, when the second clown protests the injustice of a suicidal gentlewoman's being allowed a Christian burial while a person of lower social station who had committed suicide would never be so allowed, and when the first clown in response attempts to elevate their own profession to gentility ("There is no ancient gentlemen but gardeners, ditchers, and grave makers"), why shouldn't the first clown convey the serious nature of this exchange by putting down his spade to address his companion directly, and resume digging only when the conversation turns to a more obvious bit of humor ("I like thy wit well")? To a degree the class, by asking these questions, was helping the actors to clarify the objectives and obstacles that had been informing their acting choices.

Yet another student suggested that the second clown, who has been sitting down, should stand when Hamlet enters, recognizing that he is in the presence of a gentleman (thus reflecting ironically on the clowns' recent conversation about unjust social disparities). Building on that suggestion, the actor playing the first clown offered that he should perhaps stop digging in order to pay Hamlet due respect when answering his question about how long it takes a corpse to rot, and that he should deliver his explanation about a tanner's hide with more pride in his profession than he had done thus far. On further consideration, the actor decided that his comment about "pocky corpses" should no longer be delivered to his companion as a sly aside about syphilis, but rather more authoritatively to Hamlet as a proof of his professional expertise. Suggestions by the audience, therefore, urged the actors to alter the tone of the scene from knowing or ironic humor to a humor that emerges largely from the gravediggers' literalism and blunt seriousness of purpose. The actors incorporated many of these suggestions into their final performance.

The give and take between the actors and their peer audiences at these unit rehearsals generated an excitement we would never have anticipated at the beginning of the course. Student evaluations unfailingly mentioned unit rehearsals as the culmination of what they had learned. To quote from a few: "Doing unit rehearsals before performing final scenes was incredibly helpful with memorization and developing our understanding of the material"; "Going over units in class was very valuable as it allowed for immediate feedback in the early stages of developing our scenes in rehearsal"; "Performing units in class was really helpful in getting feedback and adjusting our scenes before they were performed"; "I loved the constructive sessions with units in front of the class because I learned so much from them." Such give and take, however, would not have been possible without an acquisition of the kinds of skills that professional actors use in their rehearsal process. By the end of the course, students were demonstrating an understanding of how dramaturgical work on a Shakespeare text can enrich the potentials of performance; of how to embody character theatrically; of the importance of voice, diction, and projection; of performative language and gesture; and of the need to identify given circumstances, objectives, and obstacles—skills that would be alien to most students in a more traditional Shakespeare class, even one in which students are asked to "get on their feet" and perform scenes. What was sacrificed in this semester-long course was coverage. Students read a few sonnets and some acting texts, literary criticism, source studies, and historical material, but only three plays—scarcely half the number they would typically read in a class devoted to the plays as literature. What they gained, however, was a deeper knowledge of how actors, through an assiduous rehearsal process, make Shakespeare their own as they bring the plays to life in performance; and, confident in that knowledge, they exhibited a pride in their ownership of Shakespeare that we had never before, in our decades of teaching, witnessed in students.

## Notes

1 For an intriguing discussion of how using theatre-based techniques in the classroom allows students to investigate their diverse identities, see Ayanna Thompson and Laura Turchi's chapter on "Embodiment: What is it (not)?" in *Teaching Shakespeare with Purpose: A Student-Centred Approach* (London: Bloomsbury, 2016), 69–96. See also Fiona Banks, *Creative Shakespeare: The Globe Education Guide to Practical Shakespeare* (London: Bloomsbury, 2014).

2 Textbooks which emphasize Stanislavski's use of action analysis include Uta Hagen and Haskel Frankel's *Respect for Acting* (New York: Macmillan Publishing, 1974), 145–190; Sonia Moore's *The Stanislavski System* (New York: Penguin Books, 1984), 3–45; and Stilson, Clark, and McGaw's *Acting is Believing* (Stamford, CT: Cengage Learning, 2015), 19–82.

# 6

# "Performing *Hamlet*": Repeated Visits to Elsinore

## *Russell Jackson*

I devised "Performing *Hamlet*" as an optional final-year
module in the Department of Drama and Theatre Arts at the
University of Birmingham (UK). From September 2009 it
ran once in each academic year until I retired from teaching
in April 2018. ("Module" is the term used here for part of
a degree course: the relationship corresponds to "course"
and "program" respectively in the nomenclature common in
North American institutions.) It was devised as an optional
module combining practical and theoretical elements, in a
department where the "options" added to core elements were
for the most part *either* practice- *or* theory-based.

By 2009 I had been involved as a text consultant,
working with directors and actors, on several productions
of the play, including film and radio versions directed by
Kenneth Branagh and the stage production directed by
Michael Grandage, with Jude Law as the prince. (More
recently, in September 2017, I was in the creative team
for another production by Branagh, this time with Tom
Hiddleston in the title part.) My first experience of the play
as an audience member was in 1966, when I saw the revival
of Peter Hall's 1965 Royal Shakespeare Theatre production,
with David Warner, so that one way and another I had been
knocking around Elsinore for five decades. The impetus
behind the module was my desire to draw on this experience

of the play in a way that would focus students on some of the play's myriad opportunities and choices. This would not be a production, so there would be certain limitations: in-depth exploration of individual characters by actors and the pursuit of a distinctive directorial vision would be out of the question. There would also be freedoms that resulted from these limitations: we would be able to play the scenes and play with the scenes in the kind of open rehearsal that productions can rarely afford. Perhaps "workshop" is the proper term to use here. The directors I have worked with have favoured a minimal amount of table work before "getting the play on its feet," but their productions have been preceded by discussions with individual actors as well as the other members of the team.

I set myself a rule for the sessions: I would never say "When we did it with such-and-such an actor ..." My credentials as a *Hamlet* habitué would not be on show. There were times when this did happen, especially when students used scenes from Branagh's film for discussion, but I was anxious to keep the play free of any semblance of authorita-tive pronouncement on my part. In the event, students have frequently shown me possibilities that I had not expected, and this corresponds to my experience of productions. My favourite metaphor for this is that of a large country house, a stately home that one has visited repeatedly, finding a new room or passage or even a whole wing that one didn't dis-cover on the last visit.

Another, perhaps more important, reason for devising and teaching "Performing *Hamlet*" was the need for more options involving close textual work within the department's syllabus, and creating the experience of intimacy with one play over a longish period. Ten two-hour sessions would not be the same as an intensive three- or four-week rehearsal period of the kind that leads up to most British theatre productions, but it would be different from the kinds of engagement with a single text possible in other modules. *Hamlet* was a good choice because of the range of alternatives it presents, as well as its status as a major work. Students would probably have encountered it already in the theatre, on screen, or in the classroom before coming to university, and many in fact turned out to have seen more than one production or even taken part in one, but the module proposed an unusual way of approaching the play. Its advantages and drawbacks will be considered in due course, but first it is important to give an outline of the module and the way it worked.

Given that the assessments for such modules are composed of student presentations during the term and an essay written after it, the percentage of the overall mark allocated to each component had to be carefully formulated. In this case the presentation/essay split was 25/75 percent, and the 3,500-word essay was the principal focus for students' secondary reading and research, while the week-by-week reading consisted chiefly of the scenes being discussed and rehearsed. The most recent version of the module description as posted online will make the procedure clear. The eleven-week teaching term consists of ten two-hour classes, divided by a "reading week" after the first five:

> In the first half of the term we will be working through selected scenes and speeches in detail, with particular attention to their technical demands (e.g. verse-speaking, staging questions) and to their integration in the play as a whole.
>
> After reading week the module will consider the playing of these elements in a variety of available recorded performances. These performances and their choices will be examined in their social and historical context.

The first five sessions consisted of work with the whole class, led by me, on such scenes as the opening of 1.2 (the first court scene), the Laertes/Ophelia/Polonius dialogue in 1.3, and Hamlet's first encounter with Rosencrantz and Guildenstern. The module benefited from the availability on DVD or YouTube of major TV versions of the play, including those with the Hamlets of Maxine Peake, David Tennant, Kevin Kline, and Richard Burton. It was clear that some

students found these more approachable for their own analysis than the feature-film *Hamlet* productions, possibly
because of common assumptions regarding the expertise
necessary for dealing with cinema versions. (No, you don't
need to have followed a Film Studies course to be a discerning
and critically acute moviegoer.)

The presentations in weeks six to eleven, which in
modules of another kind would effectively be mini-lectures
delivered by one or more students as a starting-point for
discussion, were unusual in that they involved a significant
element of student-led "rehearsal" of a short segment of a
scene. The instructions given to students suggest the nature
of the task:

> Each presentation is a joint effort [by a pair of students],
> looking at the script and the choices, opportunities and
> difficulties it presents, and at the way the scene in the
> performance deals with them. You should take a short
> section (i.e., a shorter section than the whole scene) and
> suggest an approach to directing it, using other students
> as actors.

Given that each presentation could occupy no more than 45–
50 minutes, the account of each film or DVD version would
necessarily be brief, and the "rehearsal" element would take
up most of the available time.

For students pursuing a joint degree with English
Literature—in many British universities degrees spanning
more than one discipline are a relative rarity—the absence
of week-by-week reading assignments of critical work
was sometimes offputting. During the term I insisted that
proper preparation for each week's scenes was essential,
but should concentrate on the information provided by one
of the sophisticated scholarly editions of the play: simply
re-reading the text in a *Complete Works* was not appropriate. During the sessions we used the cut text that had
been prepared for Grandage's 2008 production, but as we
went along, students were expected to identify where and
why the cuts had been made in this as well as in the other

versions: how the play has been prepared for performance is, after all, a major aspect of its history. I have seen and enjoyed "uncut" performances and, indeed, participated in the production of two—Branagh's film and the 1993 BBC radio recording—but I hold no particular brief for what actors used to call the "eternity" version.

Although the week-by-week progression of the module did not call for "set" reading tasks, three books were recommended as points of reference: Harley Granville Barker's *Preface* to the play, John Dover Wilson's *What Happens in "Hamlet,"* and Michael Pennington's *"Hamlet": a User's Guide*. Other critical reading, some of it of a more theoretical or historical kind, was included in the reading list, but these books, with their pragmatic approach to how the play works (or *can* work), have in my experience proved invaluable in the context of rehearsal. Marvin Rosenberg's *The Masks of "Hamlet,"* with its cornucopia of examples of production choices, has also been a valuable point of reference, but only after one's own event: a reminder of how many actors and directors have been there before. The late John Barton's illuminating *Playing Shakespeare*—the book and the videos of the television programmes—were also recommended. (Some students had already encountered these.)

This leads to a major factor in the appeal of the module—its limitations will be discussed presently—and to the experience it provided for both students and teacher. I have been fascinated by the number of times the same questions have come up in rehearsal and in the classroom. *Hamlet*, perhaps more than many other plays, becomes a series of "what if" situations. We always started with the play's second scene, partly because unlike the first scene it does not raise technical questions about special effects and also includes much less exposition. The choices to be made in the first part of the scene range from how "war-like" the state should seem to how effective the king's declarations of sincerity may be and how Gertrude responds to his performance of statesmanship. (Recently the demeanour of the First Ladies of successive American presidents has been an element of such discussions.) It's an early example of making sure that what we subsequently learn about Claudius and Gertrude informs the actors' work but does not preempt the audience's responses, which we must assume will be "naïve" in the sense of not yet knowing what will happen in the next three hours. (Perhaps an unlikely circumstance, but one always wishes one could see a play without that kind of foreknowledge.) The scene also allows for the whole of a student group—ideally about 15—to be actively involved and to explore the ways of creating the social and political dynamics of the scene.

Other scenes open up discussions of a similar but different nature. The first act's third scene reveals the limitations of treating Polonius as a "tedious old fool" (don't take Hamlet's word for it) or simply as a tyrannical parent (after all, Ophelia's grief at his death is a major factor in her madness). This is probably the other aspect of the play that makes it appropriate for this kind of approach: it challenges easy assumptions at every turn. A first-year student once told me after a lecture on Aristotle's *Poetics* that he was worried because he didn't *quite* understand what was meant by "catharsis," which prompted the reflection that he should not worry too much, as he was joining a club with a very illustrious membership. *Hamlet* is an even more useful example from this point of view, an exhilarating reminder that there aren't correct answers, and that the open-ended nature of informed academic enquiry rather than the furnishing of approved wisdom is the proper business of education. This may seem a rather grand claim for what is, after all, only a module, but it's consistent with the approach of the whole syllabus of which it was a part.

The quasi-rehearsal mode fostered this through its attention to such basic factors as asking what a given character expects from a scene and whether they achieve it; what transactions take place; and how the language supports and, to some extent, directs the actors. The last of these sometimes called for a certain amount of demystification, allaying apprehensions about verse and drawing attention (with great help from John Barton) to the ways in which meter and rhetorical organization—notably the use of antithesis—are accessible and vital sources of strength in the actor's performance. There was no way in which the module would encompass the kind of training that actors receive either at drama schools or in such companies as the RSC, but this work on *Hamlet* was a way of introducing some basics. The module emphasized direction rather than acting in itself, and ability as an actor was not a prerequisite: some of the most interesting and valuable contributions came from students who had no particular interest in being performers. This being a department of drama and theatre arts, there was of course no shortage of aspiring actors, but the module was not designed to privilege them.

If I consider the aspects of the module that were not as satisfying as I could have wished, from an academic point of view the relative lack of attention to critical commentary on the play would seem to be the most important. In an ideal world, with the duration not restricted to ten two-hour sessions, this would have been developed alongside the practical work rather than being postponed until the essays were written during the vacation immediately following the run of the module. On the other hand, the research done by students for their presentations, although limited, was often very impressive. But this raises another problem: assessment. The department's established (and published) criteria for "practical" modules and those for theoretical and historical work overlap but do not correspond directly to one another. More important, in "practical" modules, such as those on devising and similar topics, presentations typically would be given by groups of students in a session at the end of the module's run. This arrangement is also convenient for the monitoring of the assessment procedure, a process required by the university in which colleagues sample the work done: if the presentations are given over a period of weeks, the workload for a member of staff as second marker becomes unfeasible. We managed to deal with this by carefully targeting the sessions to be attended and by making sure the scripts and preparatory work of each presentation, which are submitted online and in person, were available to the second marker.

The absence of the responsibilities and opportunities of a full production was not really a problem, and (as I have suggested already) gave the module a degree of freedom that was welcomed. In fact, it proved a popular choice, and the fact that, to put it simply, we had *fun* with a great tragedy was liberating for many students. This was reflected in the students' own module assessments, qualified by some comments on the lack of a weekly reading assignment. In some cases it was obvious that students had expected a more formally "academic" approach.

On the whole, this was a successful and effective module, and for me a valuable element of my experience of the play. However, one difference between "real" rehearsal and that used in this module remains to be mentioned. Theatre companies, defined as a group of actors and a "creative team" (in which I would insist on including stage management) assembled for a particular production, become temporary families, with an *esprit de corps* that usually if not invariably prevails over other concerns in the drive towards performance. I have experienced membership of such families in varying sizes, with projects of varying duration, from seven days to rehearse and record a radio version of the "full" text of *Hamlet* to sixty days in the studios for the feature film of the same text. A cohort of third-year drama students brings its own social dynamic to a study option, usually but not always fully informed by professionalism, and the task in hand does not really shape the group's relationships. This is not cited by way of discouragement to anyone contemplating but not yet committed to a similar project—but it is worth bearing in mind. There are no auditions, and it is the students rather than the tutor who create the group's membership. It's a tribute to the talent and commitment of the greater number of those who took the module that it has been a pleasure to teach. The fact that, for my own part, I didn't set out to test or prove an over-arching view of the play or its characters has been a distinct advantage. After all, Shakespeare's Elsinore is always worth the detour and never ceases to surprise.

# 7

# "Gladly Would He Learn and Gladly Teach": Empowering Students with Shakespeare

## Sidney Homan

When I got out of graduate school, I naturally modeled my teaching after my professors. They lectured; I listened. In seminar we would discuss the play as a literary document or dramatic poetry, focusing on characterization, structure, themes, and the play as a mirror for Shakespeare's times. When I became a teacher, there was a clear division between what I did in class and what I did onstage and, I must admit, between teacher and student. I kept my directing and acting projects totally separate. Once I naively asked a senior colleague, "What's your favorite Shakespearean play you've seen performed?" His reply: "I've never seen a performance of Shakespeare. Why would I want some director's opinion to influence my own?" His response only reinforced this dichotomy; my worlds remained intact.

### Sharing the Lecture with a Student

That is, until the day a tall, handsome African American student, DaJuan Johnson, got up from the back row and strode with the confidence of youth down toward the lectern. I was lecturing on the topic "Why does Iago do what he does?"[1] What is his objective, as stated or unconscious, in wanting to separate the married couple? Is he driven by some force hidden deep within him; is he the Freudian Id to Desdemona's Superego; is he a vestige of the Vice Figure from medieval morality plays; or perhaps Shakespeare's portrait of the demonic artist, imposing a story of adultery on a ground-breaking marriage?

I started with the easy answer: Iago is enraged at not being promoted as Othello's lieutenant, and he suspects that the Moor has had sex with his wife Emilia. I wanted to discount the latter reason; after all, even for Iago this charge of adultery is ambiguous, less than convincing: he knows "not if 't be true," yet he will act "for surety" on the "mere suspicion" (1.3.429–432). Even he admits, "I am not what I am," (1.1.64). The motives of lack of promotion and being cuckolded were, I claimed, just a smoke screen designed by Iago, but then I was suddenly interrupted.

"What if Iago is telling the truth about Othello and Emilia?" DaJuan called out from halfway down the aisle. Admittedly, I was somewhat shocked at his presumption, but the teacher in me responded, "Now, DaJuan, how can we believe anything he says? And why would Othello prefer Emilia to Desdemona?" He was ready for me. "Sid, it doesn't have to be true. What about if it's what Iago fears, is all in his imagination, what he believes without any real facts?" "But why would Iago, who despises the irrational Moor, concoct such a story about his own wife, even bringing in Cassio as a potential lover: 'For I fear Cassio with my nightcap too' (2.1.229)?" DaJuan's response was precious. "Maybe he's lonely. He's lost Othello to Desdemona, thinks he's lost his wife to Othello, and now he wants his military buddy back, and so he creates a fellow cuckold."

I was hooked. Soon we were going back and forth before the class, like two actors improvising on a scene together:

Sid:      Wouldn't a self-inflicted cuckoldry give a special
          meaning to Iago's "In following him, I follow
          but myself" (1.1.64)?
DaJuan:   You're right. And isn't Iago speaking about him-
          self in his false assurance that "jealousy /
          Shapes faults that are not" (3.3.74–75)?
Sid:      His truism about reputation—"He that filches
          from me my good name / Robs me of that which

not enriches him / And makes me poor indeed" (3.3.188–190)—is no less self-referential. However shaky his suspicion, Iago's observation, "That cuckold lives in bliss / Who, certain of his fate, loves not his wronger" (3.3.197–200), announces his own plan now that he believes both Othello and Cassio have betrayed him.

DaJuan:   Iago's sort of an artist, refashioning Othello as himself; both are "fixed figure[s] for the time of scorn" (4.2.65). What about if Iago and Othello are the same person?

Sid:   Or *become* the same person.

Soon the students became engaged. Someone called out, "The same person—is this what happens in what you called their 'marriage' at the end of that long scene in act 3?"

"Yes," I replied. "When Othello and then Iago kneel as they exchange vows in the campaign to murder Desdemona. Othello cancels Cassio's promotion when he announces, 'Now art thou my lieutenant,' as Iago, like a blushing bride, replies, 'I am your own forever.'"

DaJuan now had a proposal I couldn't resist. "Let's do it, Sid, let's play that scene—you play Othello and I'll be Iago."

As we ran the exchange at the end of act 3 (3.3.455–482), DaJuan and I faced the class together, directors to each other's actor:

Sid/Othello:   Never, Iago like to the Pontic sea ... Swallow them up.
DaJuan/Iago:   Your mind perhaps may change.

His Iago was the one we had just fashioned in our exchange. I, in turn, made my Othello the cuckold of Iago's creation, imitating DaJuan's delivery in tone and rhythm. DaJuan touched my shoulder, pleading, expectant in his barely concealed fear that Othello might return to Desdemona.

Once Othello reassured him, and had turned to his "bloody thoughts," I modulated my speech so that the delivery became increasingly harsh, guttural, as if Othello was now "bringing to the surface the anger in Iago," one student observed.

DaJuan's Iago watched, pleased, arms folded, turning slightly stage-right as if to hide his joy:

Sid/Othello:  In the due reverence of a sacred vow.

Kneeling, I looked out over the audience as if I were addressing some priest or marriage official sitting in the back row:

DaJuan/Iago:  Do not rise yet.

DaJuan pushed me back down, but his own "prayer" to the "ever-burning lights above" was tinged with sarcasm, insincerity, a parody of Othello's earnest "In the due reverence of a sacred vow." We rose together, shoulders touching, as if we were a single person. Othello's lines "I greet thy love ... bounteous" were those of an ardent groom, grateful, before I switched back to his general's tone with the order "Within these three days let me hear thee say / That Cassio's not alive."

DaJuan now played Iago playing the dutiful soldier with "My friend is dead." One more angry outburst from Othello in his curse, "Damn her, lewd minx," and then I softened my delivery of "Come, go with me," as if all my passions were spent. DaJuan moved closer when I announced he was now my lieutenant—so much for one of his self-proclaimed motives! His "I am your own forever" was—in the opinion of several in the audience—that of a bride lovingly addressing the groom, now her husband.

As we ran the scene before the class, I sensed an energy and synergy that, although I was a popular lecturer, I had never felt before. From the enthusiastic discussion that followed and from reading their papers analyzing that scene, it seems that this was a turning point in my students' understanding not only of the scene, but of the play itself.

I still value, indeed cherish, the approaches to Shakespeare as a literary or historical text, for they put his works in a larger, a-theatrical perspective even as they help the actor and director get into the play. But these days I teach both Shakespeare and modern drama, whether in an undergraduate course or a graduate seminar, primarily through scene work and performance. In Shakespeare, students present five or six scenes from several plays. In my graduate seminars, with my serving as director, 15 students stage at a local theatre an *Evening with William Shakespeare*, a two-hour collage of his most famous scenes.

My students are now all participants, actors rising from their seats, taking the stage with me, performing together, then discussing with me how they developed their character. Their classmates expand on the analysis, adding their interpretations of the scene and the play. The front of the classroom has become a stage, with my students an eager, attentive audience.

I did not fully understand at that time how much this encounter would teach me. Perhaps DaJuan himself didn't fully comprehend the changes he initiated, but we did become friends and later in the year, I cast him as Hamlet. DaJuan, by the way, is now in the cast of the popular television show *Bosch*, playing detective Rondell Pierce. "And I've got good news, Sid," he said in a recent email. "We just got renewed for the fourth season!"

## Teaching through Performance

My relationship with my students in class was now that of teacher, director, fellow actor—*collaborator*. At the end of each couple's scene, their audience and I critique their performance: their take on the character, his or her subtext, delivery (from tone to rhythm), gestures, stage movement, all those decisions arising from what is there in the text that enables the actors to stage that text for their audience.

Often I have several couples perform the same scene to show how different acting choices might influence their performances. I tell my students that no two couples will perform a scene exactly the same.

For example, I have asked them to take up a classic challenge: did Gertrude know that Claudius had murdered her husband? Did she have a hand in the actual murder? Does she realize that her son's "offended" refers not just to the incest but also the murder when he says, "Thou hast thy father much offended" (3.4.9)? Each acting couple chooses one of these options. We have had a variety of takes on just how harsh the words "mother" and "matter" are in Hamlet's greeting to Gertrude as he enters her bedchamber (3.4.8). Acting couples question each other on whether Gertrude is honest or is putting up a front of false innocence in her cry, "What have I done, that thou dar'st wag thy tongue / In noise so rude against me?" (38–39). But the discussion, by definition, never remains theoretical since our "text" is the performance just witnessed. All three couples usually chose to have Gertrude downstage on her "What have I done," facing away from Hamlet, "trying," as an actor said, "to keep her secret to herself but ironically sharing it with the audience." One Hamlet glared at Gertrude's "As kill a king" (29), as she desperately tries to hide her truth under a feigned question, not fooling, indeed only enraging her son in the process. Now, in having to enact a character onstage, to focus on one scene, the students really have to think about their character during the entirety of the play.

They especially enjoyed those theatrical moments where Shakespeare seems to allow very different interpretations of a character's mind-set, and of just where a character is conscious of his or her objective. For example, in the "Kill Claudio" scene in *Much Ado about Nothing* (4.1.255–329) they debated just when Beatrice gets the idea of asking Benedick, as proof of his love, to kill his friend Claudio. Is her weeping as he comes upon her genuine or faked, a lure to get him to avenge her friend Hero? Or does she hit upon the plan some time later during their exchange, but before, of course, the actual charge at line 287? The option the actor takes on this issue influences every line in their exchange, interrupted only by the sudden declaration of love when they seem to forget about Hero. Does Beatrice sense a softening of Benedick's otherwise sarcastic wit in her response to what seems to be his honest concern that "all this while" she has been weeping, "Yea, and I will weep a little while longer" (255–256)? Or, as most of the students delivered the line, does she take this as a man's chauvinistic attempt to set limits on the proper time for women to grieve? Actors who chose the latter then showed their disgust at Benedick, sometimes physically, when he piles insult on insult with "I will not desire that" (257).

The students now realized how much in-depth analysis would influence their delivery and subtext. "Professor Homan, where does Lady Macbeth's child come from?" I shot back, "Where do you think? What option would you take?" I reminded the students that the historical Macbeths had children, that Shakespeare makes them childless. Was the child theirs, but now dead? Some other man's? "A phantom child like that young boy in Albee's *Who's Afraid of Virginia Woolf*," one added. The idea that Macbeth was impotent and the child conceived during an affair before or even during their marriage was raised frequently. Those choosing that option stressed Lady Macbeth's description of her husband's former hope of becoming king as now having "slept since" and waking to look "so green and pale" (1.7.35–37). Lady Macbeth throws this disparity between his desire and his performance in Macbeth's face, "like an angry mother confronting a naughty child," one student observed, with her blunt "Such I account they love" (39)—"just in case he misses her point," she added.

I often tell students that they need to "craft" every word, that they ought to be able to write a paragraph on a single line where they combine their reading of the line with the decisions they made as an actor for its delivery. Macbeth's "If we should fail?" led to a deluge of such commentary. "He's a coward terrified that he can't do it and pathetically needing her reassurance." "I played my Macbeth so self-centered, so obsessed with my own chance of failure, after she's just said she would kill her own child rather than back out of killing the king." "I want to 'spit' in Macbeth's face on 'We fail?' (59), but I compose myself and try to reassure him that all will go as planned." "I feel for her. All through the marriage she has had to bite her tongue like this, since screaming at him any further would probably drive him over the edge." Both men and women played Macbeth as an unconscious sexist when he says, "Bring forth men-children only" (72)—"as if she's too good to produce inferior females," a male Lady Macbeth pronounced.

As my performance-based method of teaching evolved, I began to offer my students more general challenges, which they would then meet by devising a subtext for their character and then making specific choices in delivery, gesture, and movement. In the book *Comedy Acting for Theatre* I observed that while the comic character can consciously tell a joke, that same character must always take himself or herself seriously. The gap between the comic character's inadequate self-knowledge and that of the audience is the basis for our laughter. This simple but basic point was quickly adopted and then explored as students went to great lengths to make the servants Grumio and Curtis more distinct personalities in that scene in *The Taming of the Shrew* (4.11–99) where they complain about the cold and having to get ready for the visit of the newly-weds. For one actor, Grumio (whom he linked with the Clown in 5.1 of *Hamlet*) teases Curtis (linked in turn with Other from the gravediggers scene) before getting to the details of Kate's accident—"how her horse fell and she under her horse" (61–62)—as a way of showing his superiority. This in turn allowed his scene partner to play up the conflict in Curtis, annoyed at his pompous companion but needing him to learn the details of the accident. The two have a history, a rivalry: at one point Grumio threatens to cuckold Curtis—"perhaps not for the first time," one actor observed—in claiming, "Why, thy horn is a foot, and so long am I, at the very least" (23–24). The actors experimented with unique gestures, styles of moving, even accents to make the two not just vehicles for our laughter, let alone joke-tellers, but also distinct, recognizable human types. As they got more into the characters and played their comic roles seriously, the rest of the play came more sharply into focus for them.

The same thing happened when they staged the comic scene between Antipholus and Dromio of Syracuse in *The Comedy of Errors* (3.2.71–153). The master sets up the servant for a series of gross geographical allusions and puns about the kitchen wench Nell who, confusing Dromio with his twin Ephesian brother, has claimed that he is her fiancé. Along with the characters themselves, the class laughed at each double entendre. But the two actors, working with the idea that the comic character takes himself seriously, layered in a subtext for master and servant, where their laughing at this "very reverend body" (90) who promises "a wondrous fat marriage" (92) only thinly disguised their shock at this strange world in which their very identity is challenged, a world they struggle to comprehend where, as Antipholus fears, "we wander in illusions" (4.3.39). Dromio the joker and his master the straight man defined an arc on their initial carefree laughter, their locker-room put-downs of Nell, and got more desperate, more strained, as the gap increased between what they feared of Ephesus and the confusion resulting from there being two sets of twins in the same town on the same day.

To be sure, some of my students were actors, theatre majors, but the majority had never stepped on stage. Pairing an experienced actor with a novice, though, brought some wonderful results. In the grave-digging scene in *Hamlet* (5.1.1–51) we laugh at Clown's questioning of why they have to bury an obvious suicide like Ophelia in holy ground, his butchering of Latin in "argal" and "se offendendo," and at the dull brain of his companion Other's forcing Clown to do something of a show-and-tell of a man drowning himself or being swallowed by the water—free will or fate. My novice actor, playing Clown, called her character "The Poor Man's Hamlet, needing to impress Other with his brainpower, an easy task." But she also wanted to "make my audience see themselves in me—at least a part of themselves. Like Stoppard's Guildenstern, I'm also trying to make sense of a world that makes no sense, where an obvious suicide is ruled an accident." For the theatre major, his Other was "the perfect bureaucrat, doing just what he's told to do, content to lead his insignificant life." Then he added, "Except, just before Hamlet and Horatio enter, he reaches inside himself and makes that astute political point: Ophelia and all members of the upper class can get whatever they want, even a Christian burial when they don't deserve it." On these lines, his Other straightened up, spoke with a new authority as if he, not Clown, was now the dominant one. My student actor had also reached inside himself and found his character.

From the time DaJuan barged into my *Othello* lecture and challenged me to re-examine Iago's objective with the Moor, scene work has been the focus of my courses. My students in turn approach the play as actors or directors. But I've also tried to be their dramaturg, supplementing—indeed, I hope, aiding—their work onstage with all that information provided by other ways of seeing the play—the history, politics, and culture of the Renaissance, the Elizabethan theatre, the play's theatrical history, the critical perspectives of other disciplines, and—most certainly—interpretations of the play as what I have called a literary text.

One day in seminar I outlined the various ways Kate's great speech at the end of *The Taming of the Shrew* might be interpreted. She is sincere, insisting that women serve men; or she is being sarcastic, promising that Petruchio won't have such an easy time in their marriage. I even mentioned that one actor, who worked with battered women, said that she couldn't deliver the speech because it reminded her too much of how these sad victims blame themselves for the violence of their abusive mate. Then, just as the seminar was ending, I added a personal interpretation. I raised the idea that Kate is not being subservient, let alone sarcastic. Rather, she reminded me of Portia in her speech after Bassanio chooses the right casket, as she gives her estate and her very self to him: "You see me, Lord Bassanio, where I stand, / Such as I am" (3.2.140–174). "What about if Kate," I speculated for the graduate students, "speaks of a finer love, one where you live only for your mate? She has a profound commitment to sacrifice, even self-denial, that does not diminish, let alone demean but rather only enhances the meaning of her love."

One of those graduate students, Brian Rhinehart, became a New York teacher and director. Brian's production of *The Shrew*[2] had his Kate and Petruchio deliver the speech jointly, alternating lines, as well as making a few gender changes; each spoke for the other. Having moved past their earlier bickering, their posturing as shrew and fortune-hunter, they had now found a "marriage of true minds," to invoke the line from the Sonnets. My student had taken his teacher's suggestion, *entertained* it, and then brought it to the stage. I must admit I was thrilled. It also made me realize again that I may have made a good choice, for myself as a teacher, and for my students.

This is how I teach Shakespeare, for when my students feel more like partners, fellow collaborators, they can make discoveries about the play as something to be performed. And so very often they teach me and—to echo the Clerk's line from Chaucer in this essay's title—I "gladly" learn.

## Notes

1 The text I use here for Shakespeare is *The Norton Shakespeare*, gen. ed. Stephen Greenblatt (New York: W. W. Norton and Co., 2008).

2 Production of *The Taming of the Shrew*, directed by Brian Rhinehart, at the Thomas Center, Gainesville, Florida, summer 1996. I speak about this play (and my reading of Kate's final speech) at greater length in *When the Theater Turns to Itself: The Aesthetic Metaphor in Shakespeare* (Lewisburg, PA: Bucknell University Press, 1981), 31–32.

# 8

# Uncertain Text: Student and Teacher Find Their Way Onstage in *Romeo and Juliet*

## *Jerry Harp and Erica Terpening*

*The authors were cast members in a production of* Romeo and Juliet *at Lewis & Clark College in the fall of 2010—Erica, a student, as Juliet; Jerry, a professor in the English department, as Friar Laurence. The director was Stepan Simek, who teaches in the college's Theatre department.*

**Erica:** It was my own sense of alienation as an actor that first made me conscious—if only intuitively—of Juliet's alienation as a character. I was new to Portland and to Lewis & Clark College, where the production of *Romeo and Juliet* I'd been cast in was being produced. I was several years older than the other incoming freshmen and thus exempt from the on-campus living requirement. I was also arriving with several years of professional theatre experience in New York under my belt, which created an odd, insulating lore around me in the Theatre department. I took no courses with the department that first semester, so my only interactions with my director and cast-mates were during rehearsals. As a result, I was treated as a welcome outsider and largely left to my own devices during the rehearsal process, which gave me ample opportunity to reflect on those devices and how similar they were to those Juliet is forced to employ over the course of her play. It may seem strange to refer to Juliet as an outsider—after all, the play takes place in her hometown, is largely populated by her family and familiars, and uses as one of its primary settings her own bedchamber—and yet there is something of the alien in her. She does not subscribe to the feud between her own family and the Montagues, flies in the face of her father's wishes, and does her best musing and most brilliant strategizing when she is (or believes herself to be) alone. And let's not forget that it is Romeo who cries "there is no world without Verona's walls," whereas Juliet leaps at the opportunity to flee Verona and begin a life with Romeo in Mantua, even when that new life requires an effective death of everything she has ever known. So what does it mean to be an outsider in one's own play? Or to be an outsider in a production in which one plays a title character?

**Jerry:** My background in theatre is very limited—a couple of small roles in high school, a single role in college. Much of my theatrical sense came from a course in Shakespeare and performance with Sidney Homan as part of my Master of Fine Arts (MFA) program in poetry. Stepan Simek, the director of the Lewis & Clark College production, said that he wanted me to play the Friar because of my connections with students on campus; he wanted the play to be as much as possible about the lives of the very people—students and professor—acting in it. Early in the process, when I was reading about the play, I found Robert O. Evans' *The Osier Cage: Rhetorical Devices in Romeo and Juliet* (University of Kentucky Press, 1966) especially helpful for its analysis of Juliet's powerful intellect and its perspectives on the play's interweaving of language styles. Before long I realized, however, that I needed to stop reading about the play and attend more fully to what was happening in rehearsals.

As a relative newcomer to the theatre, I also experienced some alienation in this production, though quite different from Erica's. As the only faculty member in the cast, I was an outsider to the world that others in the play inhabited in their everyday lives. But I think this sense of myself as an outsider worked well for the Friar, who intervenes in a world that I don't think he understands very well. When we first meet him, he is happily collecting the "plants, herbs, stones"

(2.3.12)[1] that he is at home with—literally at home in his cell. Further, the Friar interacts with relatively few of the other characters, something that I didn't realize until I was looking over our rehearsal schedule and saw that I could rehearse all of my scenes (other than the full-cast-on-stage moments we put together as bookends to the production) with only five other actors, those playing Romeo, Juliet, County Paris, the Nurse, and Friar John (we cut the dialogues with Balthasar and the Prince in 5.3)—this in a cast of 23.

**Erica:** The first rehearsal I shared with Jerry was during the tablework—or text-analysis—portion of the process. Tablework is often where clues from the text begin to inform an actor's performance and onstage relationships; for example, Jerry's choice to read the Friar's love of "plants, herbs, [and] stones" as a clue to his gentle, solitary nature. I made similar discoveries in tablework: as the Friar finds wisdom and solace in the workings of the natural world, Juliet finds them in language, legends, and logic. She delights in wordplay, makes playful reference to Greek myth, and has a morbid fascination with ghosts, ghouls, and the general imagery of decay. I remember wondering at the time how her rather Pagan imagination might affect Juliet's level of comfort in the decidedly Christian space of a Friar's cell.

That first day of tablework together focused on act 2 scene 6, when Romeo and Juliet meet in the Friar's cell to be married. My most vivid memory of that day is of the way Jerry glossed the Friar's observation of Juliet as she enters the scene, their very first moment on stage together:

> Here comes the lady. Oh, so light a foot
> Will ne'er wear out the everlasting flint;
> A lover may bestride the gossamers
> That idles in the wanton summer air,
> And yet not fall, so light is vanity.

(2.6.16–20)

Jerry spoke animatedly about the Friar's subtle indictment of Juliet, the surprise of the word "vanity" after such an otherwise idealized, even Petrarchan, speech about love.

He suggested that the Friar's cautious distrust is a protective impulse—he cautions Romeo about the dangers of rushing blindly into love only moments before—but possibly also a jealous one. "After all," Jerry said, "he may be 'ghostly confessor' to them both, but he is Romeo's 'friend professed.' How many other professed friendships does the Friar have? And how might this one change once Romeo and Juliet are married?" I felt myself bristle on Juliet's behalf. *But why would he accuse her of vanity?* I asked myself of the Friar, eyeing Jerry with suspicion. *He doesn't even know her.* Across the table from me, Jerry and Collin Lawson (Romeo), already three years into an easy collegial rapport, shared a friendly joke I couldn't quite hear. The conflation between self and character deepened as I thought, on Juliet's behalf and my own: *where's* my *friend professed?*

**Jerry:** Much of Stepan's thinking about the production is summed up in his program note, where he says that the young people in the play die because they are "abandoned by their families, their communities, their politicians, and their neighborhoods." It's a sense of abandonment that is "more often than not experienced by our students here in our own 'fair Verona'—the wonderfully manicured, lovely, and idyllic Lewis & Clark College campus." He wanted, in other words, to access the grittiness of a play too often sentimentalized. Thus, our production would have nothing to do with the stereotypical beautiful deaths sometimes associated with the story. "There is nothing beautiful about death," Stepan said at an early cast meeting. "You shit your pants when you die."

It was a reading of the play that I was fully behind. Any time I've had the opportunity to discuss this play—both in the role of a high school teacher and, more recently, in that of a college professor—I've emphasized its critique of Petrarchan idealization. Mercutio even mentions Petrarch by name in his comment about Romeo's love of Rosalind: "Now is he for the numbers that Petrarch flowed in. Laura, to his lady, was a kitchen wench" (2.4.39–41). Romeo's Petrarchan numbers in praise of Juliet are well counterbalanced by Mercutio's humor, some of the bawdiest in all of Shakespeare (see, for example, his joke about raising "a spirit in his mistress'

circle"—2.1.24). The play shows sympathy for the young
lovers but not for the Petrarchan exaggerations that enmesh
them; of the latter it is deeply aware, and deeply critical.

As a signal of this self-awareness, Stepan, taking a cue
from *Vanya on 42nd Street*, the 1994 film directed by Louis
Malle, began the show with a short film, projected onto a
scrim, of the cast dressed in our everyday clothes, coming
from different parts of campus and gathering at the theatre.
As the actors in the film walk onto the stage, they arrange
themselves on the set, a three-tiered asymmetrical structure of steel beams and wooden platforms. The last two to
enter are Collin Lawson (Romeo) and me. Collin sits on the
floor, and I begin lecturing about Shakespeare and his work
with the playing company, the Lord Chamberlain's Men.
Stepan said that in this lecture I should talk about whatever
I wanted concerning the playwright; because he wanted the
students to take as much ownership of the play as possible,
I talked about the collaborative work of the playing company and how "Shakespeare was from first to last a man of
the theatre, like Collin here." At this point I gestured toward
Collin, and the cast let out a collective laugh. I went on to
discuss the complex relationship between the play texts that
we have from Shakespeare's era and what actually happened
onstage during any given performance, each of which seems
to have been around two hours, a far shorter time than most
of the texts could be declaimed. Thus, I alluded to the "two
hours' traffic of our stage" (1.1.12), which led to my film
version to begin reciting the prologue; around line ten, the
scrim rose, revealing the cast—now in (modern) costume and
arranged as they were in the film—I finished the prologue as
Friar Laurence, and left the stage to Samson and Gregory.

One of the main challenges of the play for me was acting
in scenes with Erica, who was a far more experienced actor
than I, and who had even worked as a co-director of a theatre
company before becoming a college student. Although my
doctorate in Renaissance literature had provided me with
plenty of familiarity with the play's language, I was, in
terms of theatre work, the least experienced member of the
cast, and it showed. Although I had taught the play many

times, it wasn't until appearing in it that I realized its density of rhymed couplets, which can be very difficult to turn into a credible character's voice. "Jerry, stop chanting," Stepan called from the back of the theatre many times during rehearsal. I had plenty to learn from all the students in the cast.

Especially intimidating were the two scenes I had with Erica alone—act 4 scene 1, beginning with Juliet's "O shut the door" (44), and the exchange in the tomb in 5.3. Because I was having trouble getting those scenes to work for me, I asked Erica if we could meet to go over the lines. Thinking that some forthright honesty would be helpful, I mentioned how intimidating I found it to act with her. She couldn't have been more gracious in her encouraging response, though of course that did not make the anxiety go away. In the course of our meeting, we discussed how I could make use of this anxiety in the scene. After all, the Friar has gone behind the backs of these two powerful families and married their children without permission, and in the first of the two scenes mentioned, he's alone in his cell with a young woman. It makes sense that the Friar would feel something very like intimidation.

The most difficult scene for me was 5.3, where the Friar discovers his young friends in the tomb. During rehearsals Stepan tried shadowing me through the scene, naming what the Friar would be seeing—the blood, the two bodies—but I could not make it convincing. On our review night, there were even a few sniggers from the audience. I needed to learn more from the students in the cast. It wasn't until the opening night performance was underway and I mentioned all this backstage that the student, Ro Haan, playing Lord Capulet—and I'll always be grateful to him for this—said that it was because my delivery was not convincing. He went on to describe his own Stanislavskian approach: when he has to play a really sad scene, he said, he goes off by himself and thinks about the saddest thing he can remember. As it happened, I had already been doing this, thinking about a high school student named Mary Anne whom I had been mentoring in my former career teaching at a St. Louis prep school. She went to do volunteer work during winter break and was killed in a freak accident, sitting atop a bus (a common practice where she was) that lost power and rolled down a hill. Somehow out of my exchange with Ro Haan, I realized that I had been thinking about the wrong thing. Because the funeral was closed casket, I never saw Mary Anne after she died, meaning that I could only picture her alive, running cross country or striding down the halls of the school. What I needed to do was rehearse the phone call that came from the school principal, who knew about my mentoring relationship with her, delivering the news of her death. "There was an accident," the principal had said. "Mary Anne didn't make it."

Waiting to go on, with this conversation echoing through my head, through my very body, I also listened as Collin welcomed Romeo's death, and knowing that Erica was about to enact her death as Juliet. Around the line "Arms, take your last embrace" (5.3.113), the old feelings of grief associated with Mary Anne shifted to Erica and Collin. I was somehow grieving my young friends and colleagues in the cast. In my mouth and chest, the language of that scene—"Lady, come from that nest / Of death, contagion, and unnatural sleep" (5.3.151–152)—felt very different, and much more real. There were no sniggers. Later, Ro told me that head after head of the rest of the cast rose as they registered that something different from before was happening. The student playing Tybalt said that although he'd heard me deliver those lines many times, he'd never heard me say them like that. "That's where the money is," Ro said, standing beside me during the bows. With his help, with Erica's, Collin's, Stepan's, and Mary Anne's, for one passing moment I was able to inhabit this difficult language, and welcome it into me, in a way that I never could before.

A week after Mary Anne had died, a letter had arrived from her in the mail, talking about what she was doing on her volunteer trip, as well as what she hoped to do in the future. Of course, that future never came for her. The letter has become a kind of holy relic. I carried it in my jacket pocket for the rest of the *Romeo and Juliet* performances.

The words of the dead indeed breathe in the bodies of the living.

**Erica:** The most difficult section of the play for me was "the marathon." This was my and Jerry's name for the four-scene stretch—from 3.5 to 4.3—which follows Juliet through the last full waking day of her life, beginning when she wakes up with her husband for the first (and only) time, and ending when she falls into her deathlike sleep. The day represents a hyper-condensed and decidedly grim "coming of age" story, during which Juliet's predicament becomes more and more extreme. Inside this breathless stretch of hardship, the Friar is her only ally, the only one who fully understands what she's going through. This dynamic was somewhat mirrored in reality; Jerry was the first to remark on the intensity of the marathon and made a habit of checking in with me during or after runs and performances to ask how I was "holding up."

While the marathon—which represented about 40 non-stop minutes of stage time—was physically, emotionally, and technically demanding, it was also great fun to play. So much happens to Juliet in that time, and yet she remains active and dynamic throughout—bucking and struggling against each new blow she is dealt. One day, during a breathless rehearsal of the marathon scenes, a new insight struck me (one I imagine I shared with Jerry the next day in his office, where I was increasingly spending time to discuss the play): whereas Romeo either submits to his fortune—"but he that hath the steerage of my course / direct my suit" (1.4.112–113)—or laments it—"O I am fortune's fool" (3.1.138)—Juliet invariably tries to master hers. When she doesn't outright refuse a plan, she seeks to reroute it, rewrite it, or riff upon it. The only plan Juliet does agree to without hesitation or revision is the Friar's scheme to fake her death.

Juliet and the Friar are the play's foremost schemers. They are both imaginative, quick on their feet, and keen rhetoricians. At the beginning of their scene together in the Friar's cell, they share a line—and grimly deadpan joke—as Juliet evasively banters with a clueless Paris about their imminent wedding:

Paris: That may be must be, love, on Thursday next.
Juliet: What must be shall be.
Friar Laurence: That's a certain text.

                                                    (4.1.20–21)

When Paris finally leaves them alone, Juliet turns to the
Friar, brandishes a knife, and threatens to kill herself—
marking the second time in as many days that a teenager has
come into his usually peaceful, solitary cell and threatened
suicide. That speech ends:

> Give me some present counsel, or behold,
> 'Twixt my extremes and me this bloody knife
> Shall play the umpire, arbitrating that
> Which the commission of thy years and art
> Could to no issue of true honor bring.
> Be not so long to speak. I long to die,
> If what thou speak'st speak not of remedy.

                                                    (61–67)

Juliet is shrewd, cutting, and merciless here. She calls
his experience, art, and honor into question, and then, with
an audacity that feels delightfully *teenagerly*, tells him to
hurry up. I relished how subversive this moment was: a
young girl confronting a figure of social authority in his own
domain, and dominating him. The line-crossing felt especially stark in our production, where I, a student, delivered
this defiant dressing-down to a teacher. If I had spoken that
way in the classroom, I may very well have been asked to
leave it. Instead, during one rehearsal I was instructed to
get even more "in his face." What a difference context makes.

In recent re-readings of the scene, I was struck by how
quickly Friar Laurence hatches his plan and how forcefully
he introduces it; the Friar is not cowed. When he describes
his scheme to her, he ends his assurance of their success with
a jab of his own: "If no inconstant toy nor womanish fear /
abate thy valour in the acting it" (119–120). But if there is
potential for a kind of competitive sparring in this scene,
Jerry and I didn't really play it. Instead, our dynamic was

more informed by, as he writes above, the intimidation he felt sharing the stage with me. In our production, this translated to a nervous and guilt-ridden Friar, already in over his head, getting effectively overpowered by this strong-willed girl.

What I wasn't consciously aware of at the time was my own performance of power in the scene. I do not mean my choice to portray *Juliet* as powerful; I mean that I, a new student and object of curiosity, uncertain of my ability to live up to the expectations of those around me—including the professor who found me intimidating and told me so—performed a confidence and assuredness I did not feel. And here I see another insight into Juliet: She wields the most control when she is at her most frightened and unsure. This is true when, caught off-guard on the balcony by Romeo's intrusion, she interrogates and then basically proposes to him; it is true in the Friar's cell when she demonstrates such boldness. Of course Juliet must be at least as intimidated by the Friar's presence as he is by hers.

Though my own stakes were much lower than Juliet's, the role, and the marathon especially, required the same counter-intuitive determination that Juliet employs. Actors are often—as Jerry was—counseled to take whatever personal obstacles are in their way and "use them." Jerry used his own discomfort, his own grief and feelings of responsibility for his students, to give life and breath to the Friar's parallel struggles. I used my fear, my isolation, my own thrill and terror of the weight on my shoulders, and my desire to live up to Jerry's expectations, to bring Juliet—my Juliet—to life.

I was as moved by Jerry's earnest, gentle portrayal of the Friar as I am by his account of his journey into the role. I notice in myself an irrational desire to protect him from my harshest reading of poor Lawrence. Some of this is due to our mutual regard in "real life," where Jerry has remained a dear mentor and friend in the seven years since we shared a stage. But this misplaced protectiveness is surely also a ghostly imprint left from our time as Juliet and the Friar. Another theatre truism: the most important thing an actor can know onstage is what she needs from her scene partner. I imagine that Jerry and I were generous scene partners to one another because we needed the same thing, arguably the same thing our characters needed: an ally.

Seven years later I can still feel Juliet with me, like a letter in my pocket.

## Note

1 The text for *Romeo and Juliet* used in this essay was that edited by Brian Gibbons for *The Arden Shakespeare* (Bloomsbury-Methuen: New York and London, 1980).

# 9

# "In Practice Let Us Put It Presently": Learning with *Much Ado*

## Fran Teague and Kristin Kundert

> And thou shalt see how apt it is to learn
> Any hard lesson that may do thee good.
>
> (1.1.275–276)

In February 2014, the University of Georgia announced that Kristin Kundert would direct *Much Ado about Nothing*. She asked Fran Teague to serve as dramaturg, working on background research and preparing the script. Our work on the show *was* teaching. First, we will discuss a dramaturgy class project—how it succeeded for the students, but failed for Kundert, and why that failure was paradoxically important in making the production succeed. Next, we will talk about Kundert's directorial decision to build music into the production, Teague's skepticism, the students' enthusiasm, and how audiences responded. Finally, we shall discuss how our re-shaping the production in terms of gender helped the audience understand the play and the MFA students produce effective thesis projects.

### Learning through Dramaturgy: Fran Teague

Each spring semester, I teach "Dramaturgy." A major assignment has students work with directors doing real world dramaturgy: directors may ask them to gloss a script for the actors, to research Victorian medical practices, to provide images of Greek vases, and so forth. The assignment allows students to see their research in action, influencing a production. When the team working on *Much Ado* met with Kristin, she gave them a variety of settings in which women took active roles in civic life and asked for a sense of that culture's music, architecture, clothing, and attitudes toward women. They looked at Hawaii after the Pearl Harbor attacks, Rome under Augustus Caesar, Britain from year 1 BCE to 1 CE, Cyprus in the medieval period, and India today. One student was a doctoral student in English, while two undergraduates were majoring in English and theatre. They compiled a background book of their own summaries, copies of articles and reviews, and images that was 193 pages long. The work was thorough and well done, and I happily gave them an A on the project and passed the material on to Kristin.

Meanwhile Kristin was working with the designers and with the play, figuring out what she wanted the production to accomplish. After going through the students' background book, she decided to go in a different direction. At this point, the background book assignment seemed a failure to me. In retrospect, I realize that it did succeed both for the students and the director. The director needed to see more information to find the setting, and the book helped her reach the decision to set the production in sixteenth-century Italy. The dramaturgy students learned to do hands-on research using a variety of resources: traditional reference books, subject-specific databases, and targeted searching. Furthermore, they learned to use their ingenuity: to find out what people wore in Hawaii after the Pearl Harbor attacks, for example, they found photos in old newspapers. Though the students were familiar with humanities databases, they learned to use social science resources, histories of music, and collections of art in print and digital form. They also learned that they had to work together, and that means they discovered how collaboration serves research. The student who was highly visually oriented concentrated on the images, the English major gathered background essays, and the doctoral student focused on Shakespeare, as well as taking charge of writing and organizing their report. Putting together an anthology of materials that ran to nearly 200 pages is a daunting task for students, but by working together, the team succeeded.

Thinking back on the assignment, Maria Chappell (then a graduate student leading the team and now a PhD in Shakespeare and digital humanities) says:

> I remember that when we turned it in, I was torn because I wished that Kristin could use all of the settings we researched for the play; from early Britain to WWII Hawaii, I was excited about all of the options for *Much Ado*. Even though I would have loved to have seen a version of the play based on one of the ideas we researched, we knew going into the project that the performance of the play was a full year away and that the director was still in the early stages of deciding how to stage *Much Ado* with a cast where several of the roles of men with power, such as Leonato, would be played by women; she wanted a time period and a place when having women in power would have been more usual. [... The] Renaissance setting works well with the play, particularly visually. I did not view the gender make-up of the cast as a barrier to setting the play in the Renaissance; audiences suspend belief when watching plays anyway, and Shakespeare adaptations, particularly modern ones, frequently have color- and gender-blind casting (including the brilliant casting of Helen Mirren as "Prospera" in Taymor's *The Tempest*). While it would have been interesting to see "Leonata" modeled after Boudica or Livia, she also works well as a Renaissance matriarch (and complicates some of the gender dynamics in scenes such as Hero's ruined wedding).[1]

Dr. Chappell's final comment turned out to be prescient since Kristin decided that the production with its focus on gender needed a setting in Renaissance Italy. Her decision led to the production's glorious set. The importance of students learning research skills is central to me as a teacher, but what may be most valuable to them is the knowledge that research sometimes does not work out as one expects. The director's decision to set aside the work that the students had done was one that gave the doctoral student greater confidence in her own judgment, an unexpected benefit, and gave the actors a wonderful space in which to perform.

A professional dramaturg's task involves coming to rehearsals and answering any questions that might arise, but I am an amateur. During the weeks of rehearsal, I simply could not teach my courses, go to meetings, and handle other professional responsibilities while sitting in a rehearsal hall for four hours a night on five days a week and six hours on Sundays. Instead, I arranged for a rehearsal dramaturg, doctoral theatre student Jennifer Marks, to assist Kristin. I did work with Kristin on preparing the script and I gave a short presentation to the cast on the play and its language and answered any questions Jennifer had, but my work as dramaturg was largely done.

The dramaturgy students learned by doing, Kristin learned by seeing their results, and I learned that I needed to have more faith in my students' good sense: they were glad that Kristin set the play in the Italian Renaissance. I also learned to have more faith in the director: when Kristin first told me what she had planned for music, I thought that the Italian Renaissance setting wouldn't work with contemporary folk music. As the show turned out, the music was not just successful with audiences, but it also helped the cast tell the story.

## Learning through Performance: Kristin Kundert

*It has to mean something.* That is my mantra for directing. When I was assigned *Much Ado*, I knew immediately that the production would include live music, so vital to college students. Shakespeare's play actually contains four musical moments: a dance, a love song, a funeral mass, and another closing dance. That was my hook for this production—the power of music. Several years earlier, I had heard a song whose lyrics startled me. I recognized them as from *Much Ado About Nothing*. In 2009, Mumford and Sons released the album *Sigh No More*.

The title song for that album has lyrics that are pieces of text pulled directly from *Much Ado*: "Serve God, love me and mend" (5.2.87), "live unbruised" (5.4.109), "I am sorry" (used five times in the play, contracted to "I'm sorry" in the song: 2.3.163, 2.3.193, 4.1.87, 4.1.98, 4.1.271), "We are friends" (5.4.116), "Sigh no more" (2.3.62), "One foot in sea, one on shore" (2.3.64), "You know me" (2.1.153, possibly echoing "I know you of old", 1.1.139), and "man is a giddy thing" (5.4.107).[2]

Thinking about the production, I had known I wanted music, and the song gave me an answer. While Mumford and Sons was a hugely popular band at the time, virtually none of the listeners realized that they were hearing a Shakespearean tale. The music, with an almost Celtic sound of banjos and bass, is made for dancing, crying, and loving.

So I began my directing journey knowing one thing I wanted—live performances of Mumford and Sons' songs—yet there was so much more to decide. The next large challenge for me to address was performing the music. I engaged an undergraduate theatre major who played multiple instruments, wrote his own music, and played in several bands to serve as musical director. We culled Mumford and Sons songs and found seven to use in the production. In additional to the four songs Shakespeare called for, we played one under a prologue of action setting up the show, one at the end of the first act, and one at the beginning of the second act.

In university productions, most actors in a theatre department identify as female. Meanwhile, the cast of *Much Ado* calls for 17 men and 4 women. Casting our production as Shakespeare intended would be challenging, as we simply didn't have enough men audition. Additionally, as a professor of acting, I see our productions as laboratories for our teaching, and since the majority of students in acting classrooms are female, it doesn't seem fair or prudent to cast Shakespearean productions traditionally. So I had two choices to accommodate our acting pool: change men's roles to women's roles or have women play men. As I am not a fan of women playing men when there isn't a concept or logical reason, I was going to need to create a matriarchal world where women were leaders both in the home and in the community. I was lucky that I could cast the production before designs were complete. I was working with a wonderful MFA candidate costume designer who was willing to be flexible for a while as I determined the genders of some of the roles. In the end, I cast 11 women and 9 men. Conrad, Don John, Leonato, Antonio, Dogberry, and two members of the watch became women.

Stephanie Murphy, who played Beatrice, wrote about the effect of that casting:

> Leonata and Antonia … represent a completely female-run household bustling with lively maternal energy. Don Pedro's arrival with a party of men became all the more jarring in light of this adjustment.
>
> Beatrice, as a product of this household, became more of a product of her environment than a rebel against it. Leonata and Antonia banter with her, and while she outshines them, their dialogue is now firmly within a homosocial female sphere. As opposed to a woman who could "hold her own with the boys" (a tomboyish cliché that I was happy to cast aside), Beatrice became reminiscent of *Little Women*'s Jo March or *Pride and Prejudice*'s Elizabeth Bennett. Surrounded by outspoken, intelligent female authority figures, Beatrice was able to simultaneously embrace her wit and her femininity because she had no example to suggest that they were mutually exclusive. In fact, it now seemed that Hero, in her silent position of responsibility, became the outlier. While I still viewed her as a moral authority, I now felt an even greater imperative to protect and help her fit in with the rest of the family.[3]

The shift to more women's roles helped the performers and led to other changes as well. I had to find a world filled with strong women, yet felt that I couldn't bring our production too far forward in time, as the slandered lady story wouldn't ring true. I also needed a world that was large and dramatic, containing the possibility for big emotions, design, and music. That was the basis of the wonderful

*Figure 9.1* Beatrice (Stephanie Murphy) on the Balcony, by permission of the University of Georgia Department of Theatre and Film Studies

dramaturgical book that Fran's students created for me. I read it, studied it, and threw it all away. While any of these worlds could have met the needs of our production of *Much Ado*, none of them would unite with the sound of Mumford and Sons' music. Ironically, the historical time and location of Shakespeare's text resounded most fully in the music of Mumford and Sons. Finding and creating a solid concept for a production involves trying on many different worlds before encountering the best option. Their dramaturgy work had saved me countless hours of research so that I could find our production's setting: Renaissance Italy.

Creating a matriarchal world for this production by changing some of the male roles to women had several unintended yet helpful consequences surrounding the slandered lady story within the text. Modern audiences often have difficulty with this element of the plot. They don't understand Hero's inability to defend herself, nor her forgiveness of Claudio in the resolution of the play. In our production, the actor playing Hero stood up for herself more than in any other production that I have seen. Of course her text doesn't allow her to do so, but her body language and physicality fought the accusation of her infidelity. She constantly shook her head and quietly said "No" under her breath. She tried to cling to Claudio and comfort or pacify him, overstepping the period boundaries of modesty. The fact that there were strong women surrounding her made this conceivable and even expected. She was not merely a passive observer. Additionally, in the scene where Claudio goes to "Hero's grave" to lament his sin, I staged the whole household of women watching from the balcony. It was only when Hero was satisfied that Claudio was sufficiently penitent that the plot moved forward and they were reunited. Hero was able to have the agency in her forgiveness of and reunion with Claudio. The audience observed a tribe of women who stood together and protected each other, which is far easier to embrace than a father "propertying" his daughter.

I set to work with the designers to create probably the most beautiful playground I have ever worked in. The scenic designer was faculty member Julie Ray, the costume designer Matt Mallard, an MFA completing his thesis, and the lighting designer Mark Stater, another MFA student working on his qualifying project. Surprisingly to me I found all my central images for our design residing in the music videos of Mumford and Sons. Perhaps that seems logical to some, but I have never before found a contemporary band telling a Shakespearean tale so completely. The designers, like Fran, were a bit skeptical of marrying Mumford with a Renaissance design, but I spoke of the work of Baz Luhrmann, who often mashed up contemporary music with period pieces, and they jumped on board.

Now the ultimate hurdle: casting. I wanted the musicians to be characters in the production and not a band that sat in the corner. Thus, I needed actor–musicians. We put out a casting call that asked students to sing and to bring to auditions whatever instrument they played. Mumford and Sons uses guitars, banjos, keyboard, bass, and percussion. Knowing that a banjo would be a long shot, I was hoping

*Figure 9.2 Much Ado* 2015: the musicians performing during a high school matinee, by permission of the University of Georgia Department of Theatre and Film Studies.

to get all of those instruments plus perhaps some others. My musical director was ready for anything. Ultimately the main "band" included Friar Francis, our musical director, who sang and played guitar and keyboard; Dogberry, the main singer; Verges, who played keyboard and sang backup; and four members of the watch, who played bass, guitar, drums, and mandolin while singing backup. For several numbers, Don Pedro joined in on guitar, Claudio on cojon, and Hero on accordion. Both Hero and Claudio sang. The main band was present throughout the show as their characters or providing the music.

The rehearsals began with much excitement as two members of the company, Stephanie Murphy and Zach Byrd, were working on their MFA thesis roles while other members had never performed Shakespeare before in their lives. The level of knowledge and experience varied greatly. I am not a fan of spending large amounts of time on table work as

I think that actors in smaller roles can feel that their time is being wasted, so after one long day of a read, dramaturgical presentations, and an iambic pentameter intensive, we set to work. I started each rehearsal at the table going over the scene to make sure everyone knew exactly what they were saying, the language structure, and comparisons with folio and quarto. I was very lucky to have Jennifer Marks at the rehearsals to answer questions. Stephanie and Zach also served as leaders among the actors with their knowledge of the language and their research. The musical director had arranged the songs to fit the instrumentation that we had, and I had regularly scheduled music rehearsals throughout the process. I also brought in Lisa Fusillo, head of our Dance department, to choreograph the two dance numbers. These numbers were based mostly on historical dance, but were a bit loose in the period style as the dance was set to contemporary music. We were moving forward.

## A Successful Production: Fran and Kristin

In April 2015, the show opened and had a successful run.[4] One reviewer was struck by the production's music, noting that "Many of the characters in this production are also musicians in the band within the play, breaking out into song at various points during the show with a hey-nonny-nonny and a cover song or two."[5] Another spoke of "the phenomenally placed songs" and "the stunning set designed by assistant professor of scenic design, Julie Ray."[6] Both reviewers went on at length about the effective performances.

What the reviewers did not notice was the effective education that took place as well. The variety of places where students learned is worth noting: they worked independently and collaboratively in classrooms, libraries, workshops, and rehearsal rooms, as well as on computers and on stage. In addition, the production was the thesis project for three MFA candidates in theatre (two in acting, one in costume design), served as a design opportunity for an MFA lighting designer, and contributed to the research programs of a doctoral student in English and another in theatre. Undergraduate actors received course credit for their theatrical work, but they also received a crash course in Shakespeare's text. Those 20 actors were not the only students affected by the production. Around 30 more built sets, constructed costumes, and crewed the show. Two graduate students and 18 undergraduates acted, sang, and danced their way through Shakespeare. In all, about 50 students and faculty worked on the show, which was seen by over 1,500 people.

## Notes

1 Maria Chappell, personal email, June 6, 2018.
2 All quotations from *Much Ado* are taken from the *Arden Shakespeare: Complete Works*, ed. Richard Proudfoot et al. (London: Methuen, 2011), 913–940. We give the passages in the order of the song's lyrics, which are widely (though possibly illegally) available on the internet.
3 "'Serve God, love me and mend': Performing the Role of Beatrice in William Shakespeare's 'Much Ado about Nothing,'" MFA thesis, University of Georgia, 2015.
4 According to the department's business manager, Steven Carroll, the production had over 1,000 patrons attend, as well as over 600 high school students at a matinee performance, grossing nearly $15,000.
5 Dina Canup, "Theater Notes," *Flagpole Magazine*, April 8, 2015.
6 Savannah Sturkle, "Much Ado About Nothing," *Red and Black*, April 19, 2015.

# SECTION THREE

## Approaching Shakespeare from Some Specific Angles

# SECTION THREE

## Approaching Shakespeare from Some Specific Angles

# 10

# Shakespeeding into *Macbeth* and *The Tempest*: Teaching with the Shakespeare Reloaded Website

## *Liam E. Semler*

What are the virtues of structuring learning as a type of game when teaching Shakespeare? The Australian "Better Strangers" project has recently begun exploring the potential of gamified learning scenarios to enrich teacher professional development and student learning at high school and university.[1] Gameplay is viewed by many educators as an effective way to encourage student engagement and creativity within formal teaching contexts. The move to gamification is partly a response to the digital revolution which is transforming not only the educational landscape, but also the neural landscape inside students' heads. Students have an increased desire to learn by exploring ideas freely and a decreased desire to live unplugged. In this context, the possibilities of online gamified learning cannot be blithely ignored (nor, of course, should they be blithely adopted).

In 2015 the Better Strangers project piloted a teacher professional development module called Shakeserendipity at our partner school Barker College. In 2016 we launched the online version on the Shakespeare Reloaded website (http://shakespearereloaded.edu.au/activities/shakeserendipity) and

invited teachers and students to try it as a way of enriching
their understanding of Shakespeare. The structure of the
online module is simple yet effective. It contains three games
focused on *Julius Caesar*, *Richard III*, and *The Tempest*. Each
game presents the player with the backs of nine playing cards
that may be flipped over by clicking on them.

"Behind" each card is a hyperlink to a resource (such as
an academic article, video, or extract of play-text) relating
overtly or in some cases obscurely to the play being explored.
For example, one card in the *Julius Caesar* game links to a
video clip from the Royal Shakespeare Company's production (2012) of the play set in Africa and a review of it in
*The New Yorker*, while another card links to an article on
how modern cities are permeated by surveillance and digital
technologies. The former card relates clearly to the play
while the latter is more cryptic, yet both provoke illuminating discussions of *Julius Caesar*, Shakespeare's Rome, and
the play's contemporary relevance. All the resources linked
to in the game are freely available open-access content found
on the internet.

The game structure of Shakeserendipity performs a
curatorial role (on behalf of the project team) by assembling
the content in a pedagogical architecture. A maximum of four
cards may be flipped in one session and the content behind
them shuffles randomly whenever the webpage is refreshed.
For added intrigue and fun one card is designated a Wild
Card and another a Tame Card with correspondingly radical
or conservative content behind them. The abovementioned
article on modern cities is the Wild Card resource on the
*Julius Caesar* module, while its Tame Card links to an
extract of the play-text on Cinna the Poet (act 3 scene 3).

We trialed Shakeserendipity as a professional learning
workshop for English teachers. Individual teachers flipped
the online cards and then engaged with the resources at
home. After a week or so they convened as a group with a
facilitator to discuss the various resources and share their
ideas about the play that were provoked by the resources.
They were particularly encouraged to embrace new ideas and
blend disparate concepts during the full group discussion.

The game structure causes serendipitous encounters with ideas and thus provokes novel thinking while simultaneously hindering any individual's conscious or unconscious bias towards engaging with familiar or favoured resources to the exclusion of others. The teachers' anonymous feedback showed that they loved Shakeserendipity. One wrote, "I love the left of field resources and how they can spark discussion," and another commented: "Not only does it deepen a student's (and teacher's) understanding of Shakespeare through its enforced intellectual elasticity, but it offers them insight to the depth and malleability of literature as a whole."

In May 2016, Shakeserendipity became the subject of an unsolicited newspaper review by 16-year-old South Australian student Dylan Carpinelli.[2] He wrote: "Although this isn't a game in the traditional sense, it is a refreshing approach to learning." He even suggested "as an addition, the facilitator can then create a quiz based on the information on the cards." Nonetheless, he declared it "a bit confusing to work out at first" and thus "difficult to get into." His review concluded: "We need more activities that are as interactive and innovative as this." The Better Strangers team took the critique on board—thanks, Dylan!—and created Shakespeed as a response.

Shakespeed (http://shakespearereloaded.edu.au/activities/shakespeed) uses the same game mechanism as Shakeserendipity, yet revises it through the lens of the student market's intuitive preference for video resources and bite-size content. In other words, in the Shakespeed modules, which currently focus on *Macbeth, Richard II, Othello,* and *The Tempest*, there remain nine flipcards of which two are nominated Wild and Tame Cards, but every resource that one might find behind the flipcards is a piece of video of approximately 2–5 minutes' duration. It might be, for example, some video art, a music video, or a movie clip, and it might relate simply or obscurely to the play in question, but in all cases it will be brief.

If Shakeserendipity exemplifies "flipped" learning (because often lengthy resources are engaged with by teachers at home before they come together in seminar meetings to discuss them), then Shakespeed exemplifies what the project team calls "unflipped" learning because no preparation outside class, beyond knowing the play under analysis, is required. Students merely come to the class and the Shakespeed cards are flipped and played onscreen in class time and then discussed in various ways immediately afterwards, also in class time. This is a virtue of the short duration of the video content. Should a teacher wish to develop the initial ideas provoked by Shakespeed they may do so by extending them in various learning tasks such as essays, debates, or creative pieces inspired by the exercise. Importantly, while the game structure and the video resources make initial pedagogical engagement easier, they require professional expertise from teachers and genuine intellectual effort from students to succeed in class.

In the case of both Shakeserendipity and Shakespeed much planning and design underlies a simple mechanism which can be used quite diversely by the facilitator or teacher according to their professional expertise. This seems to put the right amount of effort and complexity in the right places.

Why is it so effective and how can a simple five-minute game fill an hour with engaged and creative thinking that delivers participants new insights into a Shakespearean play? Well, the initial game-style fun of selecting which cards to flip on screen and then to view (via lively management of group picks or individual voting in class) moves easily into watching videos that are legible to anyone (even if containing challenging or unexpected content) and present ideas that everyone will have views on. Moreover, it is intellectually pleasurable and rewarding to make connections to the Shakespearean text from the video content and discussion around it because such connection-making is fresh, personal, and collaborative. There is an upbeat vibe in class as students' insights about the play spark off the videos and build on each other's insights, thereby taking the class in unexpected directions and setting up lines of discovery and engagement that students and teachers then want to pursue further. It's time for some examples.

Australian high school teacher Catherine Hicks shared the *Macbeth* Shakespeed module with her Year 12 class in North Queensland as part of a larger learning activity.[3] Students were to write a memoir from the perspective of a minor character in *Macbeth* and Hicks used Shakespeed "as an activity to help them brainstorm the themes and ideas and create modern interpretations of the play." She reports "some good discussions and writing about how Shakespeare can be reimagined in a way of their choice" and notes that the British Council's "Shakespeare Lives in 2016" video of Lady Macbeth's "Unsex me here" soliloquy with its "grotesque" animated sequence "is a particular favourite." She also notes that the students appreciate the game's mechanism enabling them to email themselves a copy of the links to the resources they picked.

In the *Macbeth* Shakespeed game the Wild Card is a YouTube audio clip (with lyrics displayed) of the song "Metaphor" by Swedish alternative metal band In Flames. The song's persona reflects on the pain, sickness, and entrapment of his desire. His meditation is highly suggestive of the rich mixture of obsessiveness, hunger, and disease in (some!) relationships and the envelopment of one person's subjectivity by another's. The music is a powerful accompaniment because of its blend of hypnotic melody and rough-edged refrain. As the Wild Card, this resource is meant to be a particular challenge to students' ability to think associatively and creatively in response to *Macbeth* and its success will depend on the teacher's guidance and adequate time for student reflection and discussion. Hicks had to work hard to make the possibilities come alive with her Year 12 class and I had a similar experience when I used the "Metaphor" flipcard with a postgraduate class at the University of Birmingham's Shakespeare Institute in Stratford-upon-Avon. This is no criticism of the students at either institution because they did their best with this decidedly radical Wild Card in tight time constraints. Indeed, the postgraduate students were highly enthusiastic about creativity because the course they were taking (and in which I was a guest teacher) was all about creativity and led by the inspiring Professor Ewan Fernie. Nor do I believe Hicks and I are hopeless teachers—but like any teachers we need to be learning all the time. Indeed, since the human mind is so shaped by its habits, if Hicks and I taught the same students with the same flipcards a second time, we would probably all get more out of it because both teachers and students would be developing capacities sown by the previous experience. I don't think the toughness of this Wild Card is a reason to scrap it as a Shakespeed resource, but rather to ponder how hard it is for students at all levels of institutional study to engage in thoroughly creative, real-time thinking and how much teachers have to learn about ways to nurture agile creativity in class.

The same postgraduate students responded well to a flipcard that linked to a resource where some principles of Gestalt psychology are explained. The video presenter, Trace Dominguez, explains how the brain simplifies reality by seeing wholes rather than parts. It does so by various unconscious strategies that group things according to certain principles including "proximity," "similarity," "closure," and "common fate." One student in the class started rethinking the way we automatically treat the Weird Sisters in *Macbeth* as a single unit when they need not necessarily be understood this way. Another student, Lauren Bates, wrote this about the mad Lady Macbeth in act 5:

> Lady Macbeth is at one point talking about Duncan—the
> old man would have so much blood in him—and then
> changes to talking about Macduff's family—Thane of Fife
> had a wife—which then switches to Banquo—Banquo
> is buried—this ties in to the way that the brain groups
> things together that are similar and in similar proximity.
> Thus Lady Macbeth becomes overwhelmed by the
> murders as they all merge into one entity.[4]

It is not hard to see why a video on how we perceive reality could prompt lively discussion of character perception in and audience reception of *Macbeth*.

Let's set aside *Macbeth* and turn to *The Tempest*. I played *The Tempest* Shakespeed game with a regional high school class in Australia. They flipped a card that linked to a short video called "Caliban" which was produced for the V&A Museum's celebration of the 450th anniversary of Shakespeare's birth in 2014. The video shows a slow-moving solo dance performed wordlessly by Michael Peter Johnson in an exquisitely designed costume evocative of tree bark and earth-dwelling insect against a background of ambient music. The narrative of the short piece is the gradual uncurling of the figure till his face is dazzled by a glimpse of light before his body re-curls to an inert state once again. Students immediately enjoyed commenting on the character in terms of his being (part human, part earthy, part arboreal) and his experience (coming out of the earth to the light of the sun, coming out of his shell into exposure to the world, moving from inert comfort to stimulation and even pain before retreating to closed comfort again). Some students expressed their visceral dislike of his appearance, especially where his face showed signs of encrustation with tree matter or lichens. "He's just yuck, icky," said one squirming student who could find no better words for her reaction. This unfiltered, intuitive revulsion felt by modern middle-class students was something to reflect on when it came to discussing the prejudicial reactions of the Europeans to Caliban in the play.

The conversation moved easily to discussion of how Shakespeare represents Caliban's connectedness to the materiality of the island. This included discussion of his vocabulary, memories, and lyricism, and his physicality and behaviour. All this was very good, but what I did not expect was that some students had swiftly interpreted the video allegorically and not as being about Caliban at all. "It is the island," said one; "it is knowledge," said another. Now this blew me away. They saw this vivid performance of Caliban's silent uncurling and re-curling as an analogy for the progression of the island from a state of uncolonized nature to a type of painful encounter with European culture before its return to a decolonized state after Prospero and the courtiers depart. Similarly, the video became a narrative of the global impact of the enlightenment or Western reason. This evoked much discussion of the nature of Western reason and its moral value across cultures and in the play.

I also ran *The Tempest* Shakespeed activity during an information session about "Studying English at University" for Year 12 students and their parents at a recent Open Day at the University of Sydney. It was loads of fun to divide a packed room of 50 teenagers and parents down the middle (all still in their seats) and conduct a noisy vote on which cards they wanted to flip. The whole room watched two flipcard videos: one video was an animated explanation of the conundrum of "Free Will" and the other a pacey celebration of the age-old and globally adored game of chess. I assigned one video to be discussed by half the room and the other by the other half and gave them ten minutes to come up with novel ideas about *The Tempest*.

The "Free Will" video provoked an avalanche of ideas ranging from Prospero's curtailing of the free will of all the other characters throughout the play to Shakespeare's manipulation of characters according to his free will. I bounced this back to the group with the added context of the Jacobean theatrical scene in which numerous other forces are at work curtailing Shakespeare's freedoms, such as the composition of his acting company for which he had to write (who is the lead, who is the clown, who are the boys?), the trends for particular stories and styles that surge through the theatres of London (travel tales, tragicomedy, Italian pastoral comedy, and masque influences), and the idiosyncrasies of writing for an indoor theatre (such as intimate music, sound, and lighting). This was a discussion that could have gone on forever and kept circling back to the characters' and actors' experiences in the play itself. One student noted how characters take on a life of their own in the writing process and thus exert their free will against the constraints imposed by their writer and I replied by adding that freedoms also appear in rehearsal and in the process of acting by "parts" and "cues" rather than acting by knowledge of the whole script.

The chess video celebrated the game as a political, metaphorical, and artistic pursuit that permeates popular and high culture. What was fascinating about this video prompt was the stark division of knowledge about chess: the parents were all over it, but the 17-year-olds (to my astonishment!) were very sketchy indeed on how one plays the game and what its technical terms are. This skewed the exercise, because while the students remembered the chess game played by Ferdinand and Miranda in *The Tempest*, and recognised the video's clips of chess being played in *Harry Potter* and *Star Wars* films, they had to rely on their parents to comment on the influential vocabulary, strategies, and political resonances of the game (moves, pawns, check, stalemate, endgame). This combination of child and parent knowledge was a thrill to see as we unpacked *The Tempest* together. What is Prospero's chess game? What are his key moves? What is his endgame? Is it a checkmate or a stalemate? Is the Ferdinand–Miranda betrothal a romance or a political coup or both? And what are Caliban's and Ariel's moves?

Shakespeed is not chess, and students are not exactly players. However, if we think about teaching and learning in terms of game mechanics that provoke thought while also preserving student and teacher autonomy, it might be no bad thing.

## Notes

1 The Better Strangers project is a research and teaching partnership between the University of Sydney, the Australian National University, James Cook University, and Sydney K-12 school Barker College. The project team comprises: Linzy Brady, Will Christie, Kate Flaherty, Penny Gay, Claire Hansen, Andrew Hood, Jackie Manuel, Liam Semler, and Lauren Weber. Shakespeare Reloaded is the project's open-access website (www.shakespearereloaded.edu.au).

2 Dylan Carpinelli, "The Ultimate Bard Game," *Crinkling News* (May 3, 2016), 14.

3 In these paragraphs I rely on personal email communication from Catherine on December 8, 2017 (used with permission).

4 I quote personal email communication from Lauren on December 7, 2017 (used with permission).

# 11

# "And So Everyone According to His Cue": Practice-led Teaching and Cue-scripts in the Classroom

## Miranda Fay Thomas

Every new class is rooted in a fear of the unknown. For a teacher, those unknowns will be about the practicality of getting the class going: what if no one has done the reading? What if no one is willing to talk? What if they don't listen to me? For the student's part, their unknowns are no less potent: have I prepared enough? What if I say something stupid? What if I'm the only one who doesn't understand? As I have written elsewhere, "[t]his fear of having to say 'I don't know' is a symptom of the fear of being found out."[1] This essay suggests a method that, embracing potential insecurity, would allow students the freedom to make mistakes and to think about how "performance" as a metric works within both a theatrical and a social setting. Using cue-scripts in the university classroom to demonstrate the original performance practices of Shakespeare and his contemporaries may encourage them to liberate themselves from modern ideas of theatrical "perfection" when they reconsider Shakespeare's scripts as emerging from a highly specific and practical theatrical context, one where the characters' lines are shaped and learned by a set of assumed social and theatrical practices otherwise unfamiliar to performers and students today.

## Words, Words, Words

In his essay "What is a Character?" Orgel's point of departure is that "the dramatic text in its own time was not the play, the text was a script, and it was only where the play started."[2] His essay is also helpful in disabusing students of the entirely modern notion of the "finality" of print,[3] and implicit in his argument is the need to be aware of how an early modern text is edited for readers from a twentieth-century perspective. This is all the more vital because editing so often seems to be an invisible process: a text is presented to us, freshly printed, on clean, white, high-quality paper, with tidy footnotes at the bottom of the page boxed away from the literature itself. What is presented to us is the dramatic script in full, as if the entire play had been recorded verbatim. But Orgel is keen to move away from the idea of such faux-naturalism: "what actors do, after all, is not perform actions but recite lines, and the character is the lines."[4]

When introducing students to the concept of cue-scripts, I often prompt them to think about how the rehearsal process works for actors today. This goes some way towards unlocking what their assumptions are about the theatrical process, and is a good way to point out how their assumptions are historically contingent. Most often, students will talk about how, if they were rehearsing a play today, the company would begin with a full-cast read-through of the entire script. This is a crucial assumption that modern readers of plays have: that each actor has their own complete copy of the play, and that they know what will happen not only to their own character, but to all of the characters.

As we know, Shakespeare's actors did not each have a full copy of the script. Instead, each player had their own lines written down, with a couple of words spoken by the other characters immediately before them to prompt them to deliver their next speech act. Modern scholars refer to these individual actors' "parts" as "cue-scripts," although it's worth emphasizing to students that this is not a Renaissance theatre term.[5] Scholars such as Tiffany Stern have reflected on the essentially patchwork nature of the early modern playtext:

> In a sense, every bit of a play as it was gathered together for a production was a paratext, in that every bit of a play was "auxiliary" to every other bit: it was performance that made a text from those paratexts, with printed plays always falling a little short because always an incomplete reflection of that.[6]

What Stern emphasizes here is that the script itself is far from the complete story. While it is understandable that students should read the full text of a play, workshopping the concept of cue-scripts will actually do more to get them closer to the performance habits of Shakespeare's actors. So while Stern's work is a necessary intervention in the academic research of Shakespearean drama, it is not enough that students read about it. They must be encouraged to put these ideas into practice themselves in order to personally experience, and learn from, the issues which arise from cue-scripts.

### *Suiting the Action to the Word: The Benefits of Getting "Hands On" with the Text*

The notion of practice-as-research has become increasingly popular in higher education and other research or educational institutions, of which Shakespeare's Globe is an eminent example. As Fiona Banks writes in *Creative Shakespeare*:

> A cue script exercise has been used by Globe Education since its inception. It gives us a way of exploring what may have been an original rehearsal practice. This approach is not used in Globe rehearsal rooms today. Working with this exercise enables students to identify the information Shakespeare provides to the actor from within his writing.[7]

The crucial focus of the exercise is to encourage students to "explore how Shakespeare directs actors from within his writing [... t]o use discoveries from working with cue scripts to deepen student understanding of structure, staging and character [and t]o help students contextualize Shakespeare's writing within what we know of early modern drama practices."[8] Practitioners such as Patrick Tucker have experimented with cue-scripts and staged full productions "with no rehearsal, and with teams of actors who have seen only their own lines,"[9] but a little can go a long way in the university classroom, and even working with a short scene or an extract of 20 lines or so will help students orientate the practicalities of working with a cue-script.

There are a variety of benefits in encouraging students to be more "hands on" with a text. It is not simply that it helps underline the importance of moving away from thinking about Shakespeare as a "literary" text, although this is clearly vital. It is also a way of helping students learn from each other. Banks notes that cue-scripts are "a good exercise to do with a group who are new to working together,"[10] and until recently the Royal Shakespeare Company included on the education section of their website a manifesto entitled *Stand Up For Shakespeare*, which argued for the inclusion of active techniques when studying Renaissance drama: "[this ensures] that Shakespeare is collectively owned as participants collaborate and build a shared understanding of the play—with the whole class becoming 'co-owners' and 'doers.'"[11] This egalitarian approach is, I think, not overly idealistic: as noted by Edward L. Rocklin, "[w]hen students collaborate, they sharply increase opportunities to learn because they can stimulate each other's inventiveness and teach each other."[12] Ayanna Thompson and Laura Turchi do offer a word of warning in their book, *Teaching Shakespeare with Purpose*, as while they understand the temptation to explore "original practices," "in performance Shakespeare's plays cannot be frozen in that time period [i.e., the Renaissance] even when early modern performance techniques are faithfully replicated because the audience is not an early modern one any more."[13]

Despite this anxiety, applying original practices to the classroom is of vital use to students, and they are my concern here. Even if such a mission is incomplete, it still takes us closer to where Shakespeare's players were, and workshopping cue-scripts allows us to glimpse a way back into the theatre practices of the past in as embodied a way as we can manage. Rocklin's 1995 article on teaching Shakespeare is adamant on this matter, and articulates a firm belief that educators should use the body "as a source of learning" because, so often, the classroom is plagued by physical inactivity: "this exclusion of the body is itself symptomatic of what is really excluded, namely *action* in which the focus is on people doing things, experimenting, and trying new moves. What is missing in our classrooms is what is sometimes spoken of as 'learning through doing.'"[14] More recently, Anna Kamaralli has written persuasively on how the fear of doing something new is something to be seized by students working with cue-scripts:

> The act of performing live is always a tightrope walk. It is inherently precarious, adrenaline-charged, and carries with it the potential for spectacular and humiliating failure. What is more, the rope on which the performer walks is not affixed to a comforting piece of masonry or scaffolding, but instead is being held by another person [...] This technique takes some of those things most fundamental, and most alarming, about live performance—its anchoredness in a particular moment, its unpredictability and unrepeatability, its reliance on communication between the people on stage—and refashions them as the fuel for the work, instead of merely its hazards. It also brings home the fact that Shakespeare was writing for working actors, and created his plays to make the most of their needs, their skills and their circumstances. The precarious feeling of performing without knowing everything about what is going to happen is exhilarating; remembering that in the classroom holds the potential to ignite not only comprehension, but passion.[15]

### *Hear Me Speak:* The Merchant of Venice *as Cue-script Exercise*

As Kamaralli notes, getting students to use cue-scripts themselves can be a daunting task. But with the right approach, they can embrace the potential fear of the unknown and use that experience to feel far closer to early modern theatrical practice. While Banks and Kamaralli both offer a variety of potential extracts which could be utilized as a cue-script exercise, my favourite piece to use in such a workshop is a moment featured by Palfrey and Stern in *Shakespeare in Parts*. They describe 3.3 as "perhaps the play's paradigmatic case of repeated cues,"[16] and it makes an intriguing case study for students precisely because it shows the problems of working with cue-scripts.

Here is the extract in question:

**Shylock** I'll have my bond; speak not against my bond:
  I have sworn an oath that I will have my bond.
  Thou call'dst me dog before thou hadst a cause;
  But, since I am a dog, beware my fangs:
  The duke shall grant me justice. I do wonder,
  Thou naughty gaoler, that thou art so fond
  To come abroad with him at his request.
**Antonio** I pray thee, hear me speak.
**Shylock** I'll have my bond; I will not hear thee speak:
  I'll have my bond; and therefore speak no more.
  I'll not be made a soft and dull-eyed fool,
  To shake the head, relent, and sigh, and yield
  To Christian intercessors. Follow not;
  I'll have no speaking: I will have my bond. *Exit.*
**Salarino** It is the most impenetrable cur
  That ever kept with men.
                    (*The Merchant of Venice*, 3.3.5–20)

But here is how it looks when divided up into cue-scripts:

**Shylock**
I'll have <u>my bond</u>; *speak not against <u>my bond</u>*:
I have sworn an oath that I will have <u>my bond.</u>
*Thou call'dst me dog before thou hadst a cause*;
But, since I am a dog, beware my fangs:
The duke shall grant me justice. I do wonder,
Thou naughty gaoler, that thou art so fond
To come abroad with him at his request.
\------------------------------------------------------- hear me speak
I'll have <u>my bond</u>; *I will not hear thee speak:*
I'll have <u>my bond</u>; *and therefore speak no more.*
I'll not be made a soft and dull-eyed fool,
To shake the head, relent, and sigh, and yield
To Christian intercessors. Follow not;
I'll have no speaking: I will have <u>my bond.</u> *Exit.*
**Antonio**
\------------------------------------------------------- at his request
I pray thee, hear me speak.
**Salarino**
\------------------------------------------------------- my bond
It is the most impenetrable cur
That ever kept with men.

When working with this scene, I ask two people to read in for Antonio and Salarino, each using a cue-script I've prepared for their character. I tell them that it's probably going to go wrong, but that's absolutely fine and perfectly to be expected. I perform the role of Shylock myself. As you'll see, the cue Salarino is waiting for—the words "my bond," which I have underlined—are spoken five times before Shylock's lines are over. Salarino will hear his cue spoken by Shylock, and will probably try to jump in with his next line. This works especially well in class if you both encourage the students to speak whenever they hear their cue, but also when, as teacher, you read the role of Shylock and fully pause at moments of punctuation, giving the student a moment to try their cue, only to continue talking.

Afterwards, a discussion will inevitably pick up what was happening in that particular theatrical moment and what kept going wrong in the scene, and how it might cause trouble on the early modern stage. Then, it's particularly important to close-read the full extract of the scene again and note how Shylock's lines seem to pre-empt attempts at interruption. This is what I've marked up in italics, in words spoken directly after the "fake" cues: "Speak not against," "thou call'st me dog before thou hadst a cause," "I will not hear you speak," "and therefore speak no more." Each time, Shylock is responding to someone trying to speak over him. Which means Shakespeare is fully expecting the actor playing Salarino to speak his cue too early, and is writing Shylock lines which talk over this. The poor player Salarino is cued to say his next line—and then is promptly denied the chance to say it. And this happens over, and over, and over, and over, and over again. But with Shylock exiting, he can finally say what he thinks: "It is the most impenetrable cur / That ever kept with men." And this is Shakespeare's punch line to this long and convoluted joke at Salarino's expense: all he wanted to say in the first place was that Shylock was impenetrable: in other words, impossible to interrupt. Which, as we've just seen, he is. Salarino's point has been proven—albeit in a very elaborate metatheatrical way. Palfrey and Stern touch upon this in their reading of the scene, arguing that "[c]ues can be an integral constituent of characterization, and of no one is this truer than Shylock."[17] However, a class discussion would bring out a wider array of nuance. Where Palfrey and Stern see this moment as "a classic case of Shylock's refusal to listen,"[18] it is more accurately in performance a far more pertinent example of the Jew being talked over by the Christians who assume they know better than him.

One final thing to ask students to consider is the dramatic tension that this moment creates onstage, not just between the characters, but between the actors themselves. Given that Shakespeare's actors would not have had the benefit of weeks of rehearsal together before they perform this play to a paying audience, the awkwardness, frustration, and possibly anger of not being able to say your lines onstage is very real indeed. But, oddly enough, this confusion might even be to the actors' advantage. Salarino is *supposed* to be frustrated and angry with Shylock. And with the actor playing Shylock giving him good reason to hate him by messing up the cues, the tension between the actors manifests itself as tension between the characters. In other words, by getting it wrong, they end up getting it right, and create a scene full of genuine frustration and distress. Which is the sort of realism that's rather welcome in what would, by our modern standards, be an underprepared performance with little to no full rehearsal.

Throughout this chapter I've argued for the use of cue-scripts in the university classroom because I think they bring up three main issues which help students think about Shakespearean plays. First, it helps them understand that early modern scripts are shaped by the theatre practices of the day. Be it the specific theatre spaces Shakespeare is writing for, the actors he knows will play his roles, or the sheer practicality of using cue-scripts, the plays are not just influenced but moulded by these concerns. Second, sometimes Shakespeare plays with this for meta-theatrical irony. While I've focused on the example in *The Merchant of Venice* 3.3, there are plenty more to be found (for instance, you may wish to close-read *A Midsummer Night's Dream* 3.1 when Flute and Bottom are mis-managing their cues). Finally, re-creating cue-scripts can help us get closer to early modern performance. Using original practices—in this case, cue-scripts—can help us re-create the techniques and methods adopted by Shakespeare's company and enable us to see details in his work almost hidden in plain sight.

## Notes

1  Miranda Fay Thomas, "The 'Fear of Being Found Out': Crises of Confidence Among First Year Undergraduates and First Time Teachers," *Higher Education Research Network Journal* 10 (2015), 72–81, 73. The text for *The Merchant of Venice* is the Arden edition by John Drakakis (New York and London: Bloomsbury/ Methuen, 2010).
2  Stephen Orgel, "What is a Character?", in *The Authentic Shakespeare and Other Problems of the Early Modern Stage* (London and New York: Routledge, 2002), 7–13, 7.
3  Orgel, 7
4  Orgel, 8.

5 Fiona Banks, *Creative Shakespeare: The Globe Education Guide to Practical Shakespeare* (London: Bloomsbury Arden Shakespeare, 2017 [2013]), 157.
6 Tiffany Stern, *Documents of Performance in Early Modern England* (Cambridge: Cambridge University Press, 2009), 256. See also Stern's *Shakespeare in Parts* (2007, with Simon Palfrey).
7 Fiona Banks, *Creative Shakespeare: The Globe Education Guide to Practical Shakespeare* (London: Bloomsbury Arden Shakespeare, 2017 [2013]), 156.
8 Banks, 156.
9 Anna Kamaralli, "Teaching with Cue Scripts: Making the Most of Fear in the Student Actor," in Kate Flaherty, Penny Gay, and L. E. Semler (eds.), *Teaching Shakespeare Beyond the Centre: Australasian Perspectives* (Palgrave, 2013), 169–179, 172.
10 Banks, 167.
11 Royal Shakespeare Company, *Stand Up for Shakespeare: A Manifesto for Shakespeare in Schools*, 3, although this manifesto has since been deleted from their website. This quotation from the manifesto is cited in Ayanna Thompson and Laura Turchi, *Teaching Shakespeare with Purpose: A Student-Centred Approach* (London: Bloomsbury Arden Shakespeare, 2016), 53.
12 Edward L. Rocklin, "Shakespeare's Script as a Cue for Pedagogic Invention," *Shakespeare Quarterly* 42(2) (summer 1995), 135–144, 137.
13 Thompson and Turchi, 104.
14 Rocklin, 137.
15 Kamaralli, 169, 179.
16 Palfrey and Stern, 200.
17 Palfrey and Stern, 192.
18 Palfrey and Stern, 201.

# 12

# Collaborating with Shakespeare

## *Frederick Kiefer*

Under the rubric "Advanced Shakespeare," I teach a pair of courses intended chiefly for junior and senior English majors, though some theatre students enroll as well. The first course studies the playwright's career in the 1590s, culminating in *Hamlet*; the second treats the later plays. In addition to exams, both courses require a paper, generally at least five pages long. So that students will not spin their wheels in futile searching, I usually provide three or four prospective topics; students may also select topics of their own as long as they inform me in advance.

In recent years I have grown dissatisfied with the quality of the essays, perhaps because the writing skills of my students seem to be in decline, perhaps because students seem not much invested in what they write about and thus produce lackluster results. So I decided to change the nature of the writing assignment. Although students still have the option of writing a conventional paper, complete with footnotes, bibliography, and other apparatus, I have begun an experiment: what might be called a "creative" option. Students are invited to write the dialogue for a scene of their own invention (in prose, of course) to be added to a play we are reading. I specify the characters (generally two) who need to appear in the scene, and I indicate where in the play the scene should be added. Since many of our English majors focus on creative writing as distinct from literature or lin-guistics, I had a feeling that those students in particular might be interested in an assignment that draws upon their talent and interests.

Earlier in my career such an assignment would have seemed eccentric; these days it feels right. After all, I am not trying to produce clones of my academic self. Virtually none of my undergraduates, at least on the collegiate level, aspire to a career in academe. And fewer students at my uni-versity are enrolled in the humanities than ever before. My department has lost a third of its majors in the past half dozen years. The last thing my students need is to produce the kind of essay that used to find its way into academic journals. "Business as usual" just does not seem appropriate in a world that has changed so quickly and drastically.

In the first of my Shakespeare courses, I ask students to write a new scene, appearing at the end of act 3, in *The Merchant of Venice*. They are to imagine that Shylock and Jessica meet after she has fallen in love with and married Lorenzo. By this point Jessica has abandoned her home, embraced Christianity, and become fast friends with Portia and Bassanio. Despite the whirlwind of events, there is much unfinished business between Jessica and her father. Her desertion of the family home has devastated Shylock, as has news of her profligate spending. From Tubal, for instance, he's heard that Jessica has traded a ring for a monkey, an act that seems calculated to inflict emotional pain, for that ring was Leah's first gift to Shylock. We are a long way from the tranquil colloquy between Jessica and Lorenzo about "touches of sweet harmony" in the last act.

In order to complete the assignment, students need to think about the emotional dynamics of the Jessica–Shylock relationship. There are all sorts of issues to ponder. What has led the characters to make the decisions that so pro-foundly change their lives? What caused the split between father and daughter in the first place? Was Shylock remiss as a father and, if so, did his behavior engender Jessica's disaffection? Could Jessica's decision to abandon her com-munity have something to do with her sense of jeopardy in

Venetian society? Such questions, far from moving readers away from the script, paradoxically take them further *into* the world of the play.

What follows is a sampling of my students' treatments.

Student Andrea's scene begins with Jessica taking a brisk walk. By leaving Lorenzo at home she will "quicken his anticipation." Shylock enters, saying that he thought he heard his daughter's voice. She reveals herself, explaining that she has become a Christian. He says, "Is that what my jewels have bought? Christianity!" She comes to the defense of her husband: "He is higher in heart and mind than you ever were" and adds that Shylock is "now but a stranger in familiar clothes." Shylock wonders aloud whether a father has the right "to command his daughter, to lead her appropriately." He threatens to "call Tubal back and have him rip the life from you. A cut for every ducat and diamond stolen." She replies, "And do you think that would return either property to you—fortune or daughter?" The emotional temperature of the scene increases as Shylock grows threatening: "If fortune I may not have, and a daughter neither, a heavy casket deep in the ground will do." What this new scene registers is not only the animosity between father and daughter but also the profound unsettling of the father's mind: "This world to me is no longer right. It no longer faces upward. I may as well stand upon the sky for all the logic of this world now." Unhinged, he asks, "Why dost the world so freely slip from my understanding?" After he exits, Jessica asks herself, "What has really changed? Was he much of a father before? No. But my heart does weigh heavier now that he is so permanently my enemy. And I must admit to silent hopes that my absence would sting him more than that of his beloved ducats."

Ariana sets the scene by having Jessica search frantically for her father so that she might deter him from exacting his bond on Antonio. When she finds him, Shylock is apoplectic both because of the bad treatment he has suffered in the past and because of his daughter's betrayal now. He asks her why she has sought him out, and she replies, "To ask for your mercy, father." Why should I be merciful,

he asks: "He spits on me and our religion. Calls me a dog."
He upbraids her for trading away the ring that was Leah's
gift: "Does the ring have no value to you?" Jessica answers
that she couldn't wear it, for "it reminded me too much of
you." The issue, then, becomes Shylock's character, especially his obsession with money. A larger issue that emerges
is Jessica's resentment over her upbringing: "One of the first
questions you asked of me is about the money I've taken
from you. You did not ask anything about me, or about why
I left. Your first instinct is to protect a precious ring rather
than wonder about the safety of your daughter." Her love
for Lorenzo seems inextricably connected with the lack of
affection that she had always felt growing up. "I am merely a
servant to you. Someone who shares your blood, yet is given
commands as if blood was never shared." She makes one
last plea for his mercy. But he explains that, because of her
desertion, "my anger has grown, and my desire for revenge is
stronger." Shylock's antagonism toward the merchant, then,
is redoubled because of his fury at Jessica.

Matt, too, is interested in the backstory of father and
daughter. When Shylock confronts Jessica in the street, he
asks why she deserted their home. She addresses the roots
of her disaffection: "I went into the home of a Christian
because it offered the support you denied me my whole life."
Specifically, "I was given neither compassion nor love. You
did not offer an ear when I needed to be heard." He takes
refuge in the material comforts he had provided: "Was the
gift of a safe home, beautiful clothes, and plenty of food not
enough?" She retorts, "That is the gift any parent gives his
child." For his part, Shylock speaks of his own past hurt,
"Antonio must pay for the sins of his and his people's preju-
dice that I have been subject to." She entreats him to "look
past vengeance." He evokes her guilt by pointing out that
she left their home like a common thief: "Why slink off in the
night if you are not hiding the shame of your actions?" The
two characters talk past one another. She complains that
he is attacking the honor of his daughter. He says, "I attack
no daughter of mine. My daughter went missing the night
I went out to eat with the Christian fools. I have not seen

her since. I only attack the traitor who stands before me." What makes this scene work so well is the way it intensifies Shylock's hostility toward Antonio. Disappointment with his daughter fuses with antagonism toward the merchant, ensuring that Shylock will not back away from demanding his bond.

The world of Sean's scene is one of getting and spending. He begins with Shylock challenging a vendor over the price of fresh fruit: "These pomegranates are smaller than those you offered a week ago, yet their price is unchanged!" The seller explains that the price is determined by demand and there's a scarcity. Shylock complains, "But it is a matter of principle!" The word *principle* energizes the scene. The vendor justifies his practices by pointing out that Shylock himself takes advantage of customers: "Do you not charge them a fee to borrow money, then charge them interest on the amount, and finally penalize them if they can't pay in full when the balance is due?" The vendor goes on to remind Shylock that years ago he had sought to borrow money from Shylock but the terms proved unfavorable, so he declined the moneylender's offer. He subsequently sought out Antonio: "He charged no fee, no interest, and allowed me to pay him back only when I was able." When Jessica comes along and meets her father, he complains that Antonio and his friends "hate us because we are Jews." Jessica replies that her father's argument is "circular," and if Antonio hates him it is because "you take advantage of those in need with your business practices." Shylock explains: "Because I was reluctant to lend money to someone who looks down upon me, I made the terms of the agreement outrageous." He takes refuge in the assertion of "principle." And "because I am a man of principle, I will hold him to it." Jessica understands her father's argument but maintains that his "principles are warped."

An air of foreboding colors Camerin's scene as she seeks to understand why Jessica was prepared to leave her father and her religion in the first place. She finds an explanation in the daughter's sense of her family's victimization. Jessica recounts the raw and appalling memory of seeing her mother mistreated in the street: "I did not understand that I was different from most Venetians until an old woman looked Mother in the eye with so much hatred, called her an evil Jewess and spit on her." From this shocking incident Jessica formed a resolution: "I will not spend the rest of my life holed away out of fear that someone might throw a rock at me or spew words of hate in my face." The social opprobrium of being a Jew fuels Jessica's impulse to forsake her religion: "I wanted to be able to go into the city square and breathe freely without worrying about the stares and snickers." The basis of Jessica's desertion, then, lies not merely in her attraction for Lorenzo but in her desire for security; in Venice it would seem that Jews cannot ever feel entirely at ease. To be safe, she needs to assimilate.

Laurel has Shylock disguise himself as an "old maiden" and travel to Belmont in order to gain access to Jessica. Securing admission to the household, he conceals his true identity; Jessica fails to recognize him. Ingeniously he represents himself as a wine merchant: he would gain the trust of Jessica in order to sell a tainted bottle of wine and thereby poison both her and Lorenzo. Handing her the wine, he suggests that she and her husband share it: "Open when both you and Lorenzo are present." Shylock's plan goes awry when Jessica stumbles and the bottle falls to the floor and breaks. Lorenzo, who does not realize what fate he has narrowly escaped, reflects, "The bottle is dead to the world."

In Caitlynn's treatment Jessica is strolling with Lorenzo when she sees her father. Lorenzo at first maintains that his bride must be mistaken. She replies that either she does indeed see him or she's looking at his ghost. Shylock approaches and insists: "No, daughter, I am no spirit, though by thine actions I can tell thou wish me dead." Jessica reveals that she has married Lorenzo. "Dost thou feel no joy in knowing that thine only child hath found happiness in a loving husband?" She asks him whether he does not look forward to having grandchildren. The prospect fills Shylock with dread. Jessica connects Shylock's hostility to the death of Leah: "Surely if thou ever possessed a drop of love in thy bosom, it died the same day as she." For his part, "I am thankful thy mother never did live to see her beloved daughter commit such a betrayal." She protests that she never wanted to hurt her father: "My only desire was to follow a faith of my choosing and to love Lorenzo as wife." Knowing how her father would probably react, she "gave my heart pause many a time." Shylock seems to soften at his daughter's words: "Keep whatever diamonds and ducats thou have left of mine, keep thy husband and happiness. But pray keep this memory of thy father's forgiveness." Lorenzo is skeptical: "surely this is but a trick." Jessica, however, takes her father's reconciliation at face value, observing that his former vitriol has been "washed over with sorrow."

Belicia's new scene, filled with distress, begins with Shylock wandering in torment over his loss. He sees his daughter in the street and chases after her. She expresses her wish for "my own life of joy." But Shylock demands what he calls "accountability." Lorenzo hears the commotion and comes to her defense. She affirms their love: "Lorenzo loves me! And I him!" Shylock resorts to violence, slapping her and knocking her to the ground. Responding in kind, Lorenzo threatens to strike Shylock, who complains that his daughter has "betrayed" all that she was. He wishes her dead. What is most impressive about this new scene is the skill with which Belicia has conveyed the power of the characters' emotions. Everything is at a high pitch. Passion springs off the page.

Ryan invents an entirely new incident. Jessica recalls that her mother kept a diary. She has the uncanny feeling that, if she could somehow read it, she would better understand her situation. She believes that Leah could not really have loved her father. Now she wants proof. To this end Jessica returns home to look for the diary, knowing that her mother had hidden it under the floorboards: "I just know the salvation I seek lies within those pages." At this moment Shylock enters, searching for his balances. Furious at finding her, he says, "I'd chop your hands off myself if it weren't my own blood that would spill out." Jessica brings up the value of mercy, which her father rejects: "Nothing but Christian concepts reserved only for Christian men." She predicts that one day he may have need of such mercy. He notices that she has something in her hands and grabs the diary that Jessica has discovered. Shylock reveals he never knew it existed. Jessica claims: "I know my mother couldn't have loved you. She must have loved another and by that love had me. You are not my father. I know it. My proof is in that diary." We never learn what the diary reveals, but the daughter's effort to retrieve it suggests how desperate she is to understand her father's hostility.

Reflecting on the results of this experiment, I ask myself: has anything been lost by offering the "creative" option? To be sure, there is considerable value in the kind of essays I once assigned: students could deepen their experience of reading closely, handling literary evidence, and constructing a persuasive argument. Still, the new essays have proved more varied and impressive than I anticipated. What I like most about them is their sheer inventiveness and vitality. Most traditional essays had been more dutiful than inspired. The new assignment has the advantage of releasing intellectual and creative energies previously untapped. For some of my students this exercise represents the last essay they write as undergraduates. I want them to feel that their ideas matter. What's most important is that they be engaged by their task. And if this goal is best achieved by inviting them to construct an entirely new scene—in effect, collaborating with Shakespeare—so be it.

# 13

# Shakespeare Without Print

## Paul Menzer

My laptop is the "Complete Works of William Shakespeare." So is my iPad. So is my phone. So is the flash-drive on which I have all the texts saved. And so, for that matter, is the 2011 second edition of the Arden *Shakespeare: Complete Works* out of which I routinely teach. Which is simply to say that all of the words of Shakespeare's plays are in my Arden, are in my laptop, are on my iPad, are on my phone. Of course, the "Complete Works of William Shakespeare" are also in the ill-named "cloud" (which is determinedly earth-bound). The point is, Shakespeare's words can be instantly called down to rain upon us at the summoning of a few keystrokes.

We need, here, to surpass our usual understanding of what we mean by "words," of course, since only in one kind of "text"—a book or a codex—do the words appear as a coincidence of well-kerned glyphs. But all of these tools—laptops, iPads, smart phones—are word processors. They are all technologies designed to archive and transmit language. The book is a piece of technology, after all, a word that does not merely refer to things invented after our birth. It is among the best pieces of technology ever invented. When Otto Rohwedder of Davenport, Iowa, invented the first bread-slicing machine in 1912, he said to himself, "this is the best thing since moveable type."

The book is portable, it is cheap, it is reproducible and has become only more so since its introduction. It has only as many moving parts as it has pages. It is much more efficient than the scroll because it is much easier to access at points other than the beginning or end and therefore much easier to mark your place. It is also, for the same reason, much more hospitable to tables of content, indices, and other things. It is even more efficient than the other great Western medium for collecting and sequencing graphic and typographic images, the cathedral, which is hard to carry about and takes roughly 900 years to build.

The book has dethroned kings, displaced popes, and overturned religions. More importantly, it has instructed, educated, illuminated, enlightened, amused, and aroused untold millions. It is also obsolete. Our grandchildren will find books either amusing or quaint to the equal extent that they find us amusing and quaint. We are living in the age of late print. The book is dead. Long live the book.

The displacement—if not the *re*-placement—of the book by digitality opens up a huge opportunity for the teacher of Shakespeare, however. After all, everything we know or think we know about the words, the world, and the works of William Shakespeare is preconceived by print. And so everything we know or think we know about the words, the world, and the works of William Shakespeare is, both materially and metaphorically, *mediated* by print, a technology and industry in which he did not work. This is to say that every word we have of Shakespeare—from his first appearance in print in the mid-1590s to the most recent collected work—is a product of human agents and the technological apparatuses of mechanical reproduction. Even if you had the 1623 folio in your hands, you would not be reading Shakespeare's work, you would be reading the work of the printing firm of Issac Jaggard and sons, which is to say you would be reading the work of early modern printers, not an early modern writer.

How does this matter? Here's just one instance. As is well known—or should be better known—even Shakespeare's *name* is a product of typographical intervention. The six supposed autographs of "William Shakespeare" [*sic*] that have been preserved are dis-uniform, for none separates the two syllables of his last name with an "e". But when the compositor tried to set the "k" and long "s" against each other in italic type, the letters could each collide due to kerning problems; that is, they jostled with the typefaces that succeeded and preceded them, a problem for which modern word processing systems automatically correct. To avoid breakage (and the ensuing fine for breaking a font), a compositor would set a neutral type-body between the "k" and long "s" in the name of "Shakespeare." The problematic "Shakspeare" would then be set in italics as "*Shak-speare*," "*Shakespeare*," or even "*Shake-speare*." The printer's habit of separating the "k" and the long "s" was frequently retained even when the typeface was roman rather than italic, so that the roman-type title page of the 1608 *Lear* prints "M. William Shake-speare," the compositor adopting the belt-and-suspender approach to the setting of Shakespeare's name. As Peter Stallybrass and Margreta deGrazia put it in their influential article "The Materiality of the Shakespearean Text" in 1993, "the standard spelling of the author's name is not that of the author's hand but that of the printer's press and reflects not a personal investment in the question of identity but rather an economic one in the preservation of typeface."[1] So often when we think we're talking about poets and poetry, we are talking about print.

And so the shift to digitality—which has the advantage of making type visible, or making type look like an artifact rather than a necessity—gives us an opening to reconsider the teaching of Shakespeare and to remind our students, and ourselves, that *every word that Shakespeare wrote by hand that has made it into ours went through the production bottleneck that is print and was turned into a reproducible commodity.* Every passage, sentence, line, word, and letter that Shakespeare wrote by hand, in ink, on paper was broken down into its smallest functional component—the letter—and remade in another medium: print.

This is all the more peculiar given that one of the very few things we can say with much certainty about the play-making culture of early modern England is that it was a culture of handwritten manuscripts, not print. And so to operate with historical precision, we might think about teaching Shakespeare "without" print. We have to understand the textual technologies of the early modern playing culture to widen the historical gap between the working practices of Shakespeare and his contemporaries and the means by which we access his works. Shakespeare's first readers—his fellow actors—read his plays from handwritten manuscripts; we read his plays in mechanically reproduced print. Therein lies a world of difference.

So not only are the plays as we have them heavily mediated by print practices and editorial custodianship, we access these plays through a vastly different technology than did Shakespeare and his fellows. So what are some ways in which we can think, rethink, and teach about Shakespeare "without print"? Access some of the materials and means by which his plays were written and staged? We might start by dismantling the autonomous printed texts from which we teach, to show the fragmented, handwritten documents on the other side of Fredson Bowers' infamous "veil of print." In short, simply because Shakespeare is, today, bound by the book, doesn't mean we are bound to teach him that way.

In what follows, I detail an approach to engaging students with Shakespeare's plays without print. The aim is to estrange them from a medium so naturalized to their understanding of Shakespeare as to have disappeared. In some respects, the following exercises work to make visible the physiques that convey the words of Shakespeare, to help students understand the ways that dramatic writing both transcends and is bound by the media through which we access it.

### A Good Piece of Work

In *A Midsummer Night's Dream*, Bottom calls the "scrip" (act 1 scene 2 line 3) of *Pyramus and Thisbe* a "good *piece* of work" (act 1 scene 2 line 13), and indeed the script is but one "piece" of the final, entire "work." Players make performance—the final "work"—out of bodies, costumes, voice, properties, and a number of ancillary documents that supplement the "scrip" that we anachronistically and misleadingly refer to as "the play." The "script" is not "the play," for the play is an event and a script is an object. Bottom calls the "script" a *piece* of the work, in fact, since the "scrip" was far from the only literary material necessary to stage a play. In the comic banter of act 1 scene 2 alone—previous to even the first rehearsal of *Pyramus and Thisbe*—we hear from Quince of a "scroll of every man's name which is thought fit through all Athens to play in our interlude" (act 1 scene 2 lines 4–5); the "parts" that he desires his fellows to "con ... by tomorrow night" (act 1 scene 2 lines 93–93); and "a bill of properties" (act 1 scene 2 line 97) that he will draw up. Later, a prologue (in "eight and eight") will supplement these materials. Bottom later longs to turn the entire play into a ballad, Philostrate has a "list" of entertainments including *Pyramus and Thisbe*, and so on and so forth. The players' individual scripts—their dialogue—will work in concert with other written materials—property lists, backstage plots, songs, prologues, epilogues, letters, the entire playbook—within a system of distributed literacy designed to enable oral performance by an ensemble of craftsmen, none of whom individually possesses the entire written "work." None of them have all of it, but all of them have enough. (The lone man who might claim to possess the whole work would be the backstage bookkeeper, who holds some form of an "executive text"; ironically, he is meant to stay off stage, since the theatre disguises the writing systems that enable it.) The play is quite literally the sum of its parts.

To focus on just one central component of this system, Shakespeare may be productively taught "in part." And those "parts" are easily accessible, readily available, and relatively easy to share with students through handouts or, better, projection. However shared, the goal is to dislodge the bricks of texts that weigh upon our students, to help them envision instead the blizzard of textual ephemera that drifted through the tiring houses of the early modern theatres.

Teaching Shakespeare in parts—and without print—opens up massive opportunities to alienate students productively from the most familiar of plays. Nearly any and every scene in Shakespeare reveals itself anew when broken down into constitutive parts. It is among the most familiar of instances, but it is worth looking at an intriguing moment from *The Merchant of Venice*, first unearthed by Tiffany Stern. The moment comes when Shylock insists that Antonio be arraigned for failing to meet his bond. Over and again, Shylock repeats what will be Solanio's cue:

**Shylock**
*I'll have my bond!* Speak not against *my bond!*
I have sworn an oath that *I will have my bond*.
Thou call'dst me dog before thou hadst a cause.
But since I am a dog, beware my fangs.
The Duke shall grant me justice. I do wonder,
Thou naughty jailor, that thou art so fond
To come abroad with him at his request.
**Antonio**
I pray thee hear me speak.
**Shylock**
*I'll have my bond.* I will not hear thee speak.
*I'll have my bond*, and therefore speak no more.
I'll not be made a soft and dull-eyed fool,
To shake the head, relent, and sigh, and yield
To Christian intercessors. Follow not.
I'll have no speaking; *I will have my bond*.
**Solanio**
It is the most impenetrable cur
That ever kept with men.
(The Merchant of Venice, 3.3.4–19)

Imagine that first rehearsal of this scene some time in the 1590s. The actor playing Solanio might be forgiven for having thought he was going to have an easy time of it. He has, after all, just one cue to remember and two brief lines to speak.

### Solanio's Part

------------------------------------------------------------*have my bond*
   It is the most impenetrable cur
   That ever kept with men.

And yet, his cue comes again and again: ---*have my bond*. As Stern has taught us, playwrights operating under this system should, more or less, take some care to avoid repeated cues. And yet here the repeating cue looks deliberately, provocatively repetitive. Indeed, after every utterance of *have my bond*, Shylock says some version of "stop interrupting me." Read in print, which is to say by the book, it is difficult initially to understand why or what Shylock is protesting. He's the only one speaking, after all. If, however fancifully, we imagine Solanio trying—as was his *only* job—to speak his line when he hears his cue, he's offering a voice that Shylock can silence. Indeed, Solanio calls Shylock a "cur," and Shylock earlier complains that "Thou call'dst me dog before thou hadst a cause." You called me a dog—or "cur"— before you had a cause; before your cue came.

The moment is exemplary, a wonderful teaching moment (it predictably has a sort of "shazam" effect upon students). It *seems*—or can be made to seem—to point to a playwright intentionally manipulating the cue system to create a naturalistic effect, and perhaps that is the case. To be fair, however, the moment is probably more aberrant than exemplary, since repeated or premature cues more often look like inattention than intention on the parts of English playwrights.

Still, nearly every scene in early modern drama yields surprises when studied "without print." For, whether intentionally or not, when broken down into constituent parts, studied "without print," plays reveal themselves to be seamy, fractional, parted things. Take a more obscure example, from 4.5.126–5.0.2 in *Pericles*, excerpted here to highlight Bolt's repeated cue, "come your ways":

**Bolt**
How's this? We must take another course with you.
If your peevish chastity, which is not worth a
breakfast in the cheapest country under the cope,
shall undo a whole household, let me be gelded like
a spaniel. **Come your ways.**
**Marina**
Whither would you have me?

**Bolt**

I must have your maidenhead taken off, or the common
hangman shall execute it. **Come your ways.** We'll
have no more gentlemen driven away. **Come your ways**,
    I say.

*Re-enter Bawd*

**Bawd**

How now! what's the matter?

......

**Bolt**

Come, mistress; **come your ways** with me.

**Marina**

Whither wilt thou have me?

**Bolt**

To take from you the jewel you hold so dear.

...

Well, I will see what I can do for thee: if I can
place thee, I will.

**Marina**

But amongst honest women.

**Bolt**

Faith, my acquaintance lies little amongst them.

But since my master and mistress have bought you, there's
    no going but by their consent: therefore I will make
    them acquainted with your purpose, and I doubt not but
    I shall find them tractable enough. Come, I'll do for thee
    what I can; **come your ways**.

*Exeunt*

*Enter GOWER*

**Gower**

Marina thus the brothel 'scapes, ...

The dynamics of the scene become clearer when studied
in part. Read in part, Marina's participation in the scene
appears as follows:

**Marina's part**

                    ---**Come your ways.**

Whither would you have me?

...

**Bolt**

          **---Come your ways with me.**

**Marina**

Whither wilt thou have me?

Look at the way the scene threatens to get caught up in endless recursion, a tape loop of cue-and-reply: "---come your ways ... / Whither wilt thou have me?" It is the actor's true nightmare of a scene with no escape, which the player is condemned to repeat without end.

The name "Bolt," in this respect, fascinates as a symbol of the scene's pulse between the retardation and relaxation of movement. After all, the word "Bolt" is an auto-antonym, self-nullifying. One could both "bolt" a door and "bolt" *through* a door; one could both bolt two things together or render them asunder with a bolt of lightning, etc., and so "Bolt" becomes a paradigmatic term, and character, for the frustration and liberation of the play's motion pulse. The point of this scene for Bolt is to keep Marina from leaving, while hers is to escape. And thus we have the play's restless to-and-fro-ness encapsulated in this moment. Compounding this dynamic are the repeated cues, which both enable and frustrate this motion. These are just two instances—one familiar, one less so—of the benefits of approaching the teaching of Shakespeare "without print."

More broadly, anybody who teaches today finds him- or herself occupying the friction between a culture negotiating residual and emergent forms. As we attempt to orally covey information from handwritten or typed notes (or from a computer) and watch students attempt to record that information either by hand or into a computer, as we negotiate as well with print-and-paper books and digital technologies, we find ourselves at the axis of four radically different modes of articulation: orality, manuscript, print, and digital technologies. Indeed, nowhere more so than in the contemporary classroom do the modes of articulation that have dominated Western culture for the last thousand years clash and collude on a more active and daily basis.

In fact, one of the challenges to contemporary teachers is their obligation to master modes of communication from the rhetorical, to the written, to the print, to the digital. To share a blindingly obvious fact, cultures are constantly negotiating between residual and emergent forms, as Raymond Williams put it. One such current negotiation is obviously between print and digitality. Guess which one's residual and which one's emergent? What's this to do with Shakespeare? Well, early modern England was contending with its own negotiations, and the playhouse world in which Shakespeare moved was—like the classroom—a particularly dense site of collision and collusion of modalities of articulation including orality, manuscript, and print (and we might include gestural or kinetic here as well). Print has a tendency to mask the mess of those modalities, to render coherent the chivvy and jostle of different means of communication beneath the self-consistent standardization of print. If we light rather than obscure that mess, however, we can offer our students an exciting glimpse of the *process* of playmaking ossified beneath the *object* of print.

## Note

1 Margreta de Grazia and Peter Stallybrass, "The Materiality of the Shakespearean Text," *Shakespeare Quarterly* 44 (1993): 255–283, esp. 274.

# SECTION FOUR

## Shakespeare in Various Classrooms

# 14

# "That Depends: What Do You Want Two Plus Two to Be?": Teaching Possibility

## Cary M. Mazer

There's an old joke about how one goes about hiring an accountant. The most important criterion is how the job applicant answers the question, "What is two plus two?" The first candidate comes in. You ask, "What is two plus two?" The candidate answers, "Four." "Thank you very much; we'll get back to you," you reply. The next candidate comes in. "What is two plus two?" "Four." "Thank you very much; we'll get back to you." And so with the third, the fourth, and the fifth candidate. Finally a candidate comes in. You ask the usual question: "What is two plus two?" The candidate answers the question with a question: "That depends: what do you want it to be?" "You're hired!"

I regularly teach Shakespeare in three different courses: a studio course, "Acting Shakespeare"; "Dramaturgy"; and, somewhat less frequently, a seminar course titled "Shakespeare Performance History." What these three courses have in common, I have come to realize, is that each of them is, in its own way, like hiring an accountant. They each ask different questions: what is the shape and effect of the play being generated by the actors' collective speech work and scene work? What is the shape and effect of the theatre piece the dramaturg is helping the director and the other artistic collaborators create? What did the theatre artists of a particular era of history creating performances from

Shakespeare's scripts for their particular audiences think "worked" … and what did those theatre artists and audience *mean* when they say that something "works," anyway? It would be easier, I'm sure, to ask questions like "What is two plus two?" which might yield definitive answers, like "Four"—questions like, say, "What does this Shakespeare play mean?" But my job, I like to think, is to ask my students questions to which they, like your successful job candidate, will reply, "That depends; what do you want it to be?"

Such is the case in my Acting Shakespeare course. There's nothing radical about my approach to teaching acting. Like many others, I acknowledge what John Barton, in his television series *Playing Shakespeare*, calls "the two traditions": the formal properties of the verse on the one hand; and, on the other, the emotional realism (what Barton mistakenly labels "naturalism") of twentieth- and twenty-first-century acting over the course of what I have called "the long Stanislavskian century." If I put a greater emphasis on the Stanislavskian vocabulary than most—that a character's energy is impelled by objectives; that the actor plays the character not by attempting to feel an emotion but by having the same objectives, and employing the same strategies and tactics to achieve these objectives as the character; and that the character grows, changes, and develops (or not) over the course of his or her "journey" across the span of the play—it is, in part, because the persistence of the Stanislavskian emotional-realist paradigm has been the subject of my research in recent decades. But the real reason is that such an approach serves the larger, almost covert, goal of the course: to use our work on individual speeches and scenes as a gateway towards developing an interpretation of the larger play.

In the modern tradition, the actor plays one unit of action, and pursues one objective, at a time. A play's meaning, I contend, is constructed from the pattern formed by the actions and objectives of the play's entire dramatis personae, in aggregate, across the entire play. (That said, it is important to note, as I do to my students, that there is no evidence whatsoever that Shakespeare consciously structured his plays this way.) Alan C. Dessen, writing about what he calls Shakespeare's "theatrical vocabulary," has demonstrated that there are visual patterns in the plays formed by recurrent objects, gestures, props, set pieces, and blocking—what he calls "linking analogues." Something similar, I think, is happening with action and character on the scene-by-scene level, and the way these establish a pattern which provides a shape and a meaning to the larger play. With the goal of understanding the larger play in mind, when the students prepare and perform their speeches and scenes, they are not only acquiring skills and techniques; they are molding and baking the bricks from which they will build an interpretation of the play.

Once we've done some basic technical voice and verse work, I make a point of drawing all of the students' speech work and scene work from a single play—a different play each time I teach the course. While the students find the action and objectives of their individual speeches and scenes, they begin to detect the larger patterns of action and objectives, and the class begins to build a collective interpretation of what the play is actually doing.

The pattern of action we ultimately distill by the end of the semester has an air of inevitability and certainty to it. But it is anything but that, for it is the product of the speech- and scene-level choices of these particular student actors, with their particular sensibilities, in this particular time and this particular place. Each decision they make inevitably shapes the next one; every answer they find sets the terms for the next question they ask. What the students discover is not the play itself, but *their* play, the play the script wants to become given the talents and sensibilities of that semester's cohort.

The Shakespeare Performance History seminar is based on a similarly provisional set of premises: that the ways in which a play in performance creates effects and generates meanings is a function of the scenographic and histrionic language of a particular theatre; that the aesthetics of reception and the ways audiences perceive and interpret meaning are specific to that time and place; and that every performance is

temporal and provisional, however much the theatre artists
and audiences alike are certain that their efforts have led
them to discover Shakespeare's true and original intentions.
Whenever we look at a particular Shakespearean performance in its historical moment, we must try to stop measuring
its fidelity to an imagined original. Instead, our goal is to
see each performance as an independent creation, built from
the raw material of the script according to the ways that the
artists of that time and place understood how the theatre
"works."

As a baseline, we do study what there is to know about
performances in the theatres for which the plays were
conceived: playhouse architecture, staging conventions,
how the passions were understood, what it meant to play
and to rehearse (or not to rehearse) from "parts," and how
variant scripts might represent discrete theatrical revisions.
But the focus of the course is, quite rightly, what director
Jonathan Miller calls "a subsequent performance." We
study, among other things, Restoration adaptations; Garrick
and Cartesian mind/body theory; the Kembles, Kean, and
romantic theories of character; Victorian spectacular pictorial realism; the rebellion against spectacular pictorial
realism at the turn of the twentieth century (and why this
was deemed to so important half a century later); the "original practices" movement (and why that, too, so inspires
its adherents); and our current postmodern moment. One
thing I hope my students take away from studying "subsequent performance" is that, paradoxically, the more the performance deviates from the conditions of the play's original
performance conditions, the more the theatre artists believe
that they are being "true to Shakespeare." Theatre artists
unwittingly reveal the most about the specific and the temporal when they sincerely believe that they have discovered
the universal and the eternal.

Shakespeare is only one small part of my Dramaturgy
course, but our approach to his plays is similar to the other
courses. A significant proportion of the class's energies over
the first three-quarters of the semester is spent in collectively selecting a five-play season for a hypothetical theatre

company. The students decide what the size and mission of their theatre is, and the demographics of its target audience. And they identify a season "theme," selected from a short list I provide. (These have included games, communities of difference, the refugee crisis, electoral politics, the dangers of incipient totalitarianism, etc.) One of the five plays, I specify, must be by Shakespeare or one of his contemporaries. I insist upon this not because of Shakespeare's cultural cachet, but principally because the Shakespeare play they select can easily be used for other dramaturgical exercises: cutting the script; compiling production histories; devising doubling schemes; determining where to place a single intermission (not as easy a task as you may think, as surprisingly few of the plays break neatly in half); identifying what scenes can be overlapped, intercut, or played simultaneously, and what props and set pieces can be thematically or functionally linked (for example, the caskets in Portia's love test and the casket of jewels which Jessica steals from her father), etc. Doing these exercises subtly encourages the students to see that performance is an act of translation: that the effects and meanings created via the theatrical vocabulary the plays employed in the playhouses for which they were written can be reactivated, not by resorting to original practices (though that is always an option), but by using the very different theatrical vocabulary—or more accurately the vocabular*ies*—of today's theatre.

Above all, what the students learn through their work on the Shakespeare play they have selected is how to determine (to use the ubiquitous phrase used by Anglophone theatre practitioners) what "story" a play is "telling." The scholar-dramaturg may be able to identify with confidence the story Shakespeare's play was telling for its original audience, and if that is the story the director wants to tell, it is the job of the dramaturg to alert the theatre artists to the ways Shakespeare used the structural, dramatic, and theatrical tools at his disposal to tell that story, and to muster the resources of today's theatre to tell that story.

But what happens if the director wants to tell a different story altogether than the one the playwright is telling?

In such cases, the dramaturg should not consider her- or himself the "defender of the text" or of the author—what Andrew James Hartley calls, in his indispensable book *The Shakespearean Dramaturg*, "the Shakespeare Police." Rather, Hartley writes axiomatically, "The dramaturg owes his or her loyalty not to the author or the text, but to the production, the piece of theatre that he or she has a hand in creating" (p. 18). The dramaturg may at first take on the job of helping the director identify the story Shakespeare may have been telling; but once the director and the other collaborators have identified the story they wish to tell, the dramaturg is obliged to help the collaborators tell that story, whether it is Shakespeare's story or not. Every performance, Hartley argues, is "self-authorizing": its value does not depend upon the authority of a pre-existing text or author.

And so all three courses encourage the students to answer a question with a question, much like the accountant whom you have chosen to hire:

What does the play mean? How does the play work? What, finally, *is* the play? The Acting Shakespeare course teaches the student to respond: "What does this class— this particular group of student actors, identifying patterns of action based on the objectives they discover in activating their speeches and scenes—want it to be?"

What does—or rather, what *did*—the play mean when the play was performed in that particular time and place? How does—or *did*—the play work? What, finally, *is* the play? The Shakespeare Performance History seminar teaches the student to respond: "What did they— the artists and audiences in that particular time and place—want it to be?"

What story is the play telling? The Dramaturgy course teaches the student to respond: "What does the director you're working with want it to be?"

Some specific examples from each course would, I'm quite sure, be useful.

One semester, the play I selected for our scenework in the Acting Shakespeare course was *The Merchant of Venice*. The students instantly noticed the way their characters give multiple reasons for their actions, or no reasons at all. Antonio knows not why he is so sad. Bassanio wishes to court Portia because she is rich ... or perhaps because she is fair, or virtuous, or wise. Shylock hates Antonio because he is a Christian ... or perhaps because he lends money without interest. Shylock laments his Jessica's elopement because he has lost his daughter ... or perhaps because he has lost his jewel casket. As they worked on their scenes, the students also began to notice that their characters were constantly assessing risk. Will borrowing money from Antonio a second time allow me to pay back the old loan as well as the new one? Am I willing to go into debt when all my ships are at sea? Am I willing to risk a lifetime without women to take the casket test and win Portia? Am I prepared to offer a pound of my own flesh as collateral for a loan in behalf of a friend? We soon saw that these questions of risk are connected to the question of value: something is of sufficient worth to you if you are willing to take risks for it. "Who chooseth me must give and hazard all he hath," reads the inscription on the lead casket. What—the characters repeatedly ask themselves—do I value? What am I willing to risk? To answer those questions, they must also question the reason, or multiple reasons, or absence of reasons, for their desires and actions.

In one of the written assignments, I ask the students to set up "linking analogues" to reinforce this pattern. One student, for example, suggested that characters, when they assess value and risk, extend their arms with their palms up and raise and drop their hands alternately, as if weighing their options in a scale—anticipating the appearance of the actual physical object in the trial scene.

Some years later I once again used *Merchant* as the primary script for the course. But this time, the pattern the students collectively identified wasn't value and risk but rather commitment, contract, and bond. The students noticed that, in the script, Shylock invites Antonio and

Bassanio offstage to the notary to sign the "merry bond," and the Prince of Morocco signs his contract and sanctifies it in a chapel offstage between his two scenes. What if, several students asked, those scenes were enacted on- rather than off-stage? What if, when Portia ceremonially gives all of her property (and herself) to her new husband, she actually signs documents, contracts, and bonds? What if the ring which she entrusts to Bassanio were a signet ring, which she has just used to seal the wax on those contracts?

What each class found in the play did not exclude what the other class had found. Their divergent interpretations were simply the product of the different answers they found, based on the different questions they posed, about their characters' actions and objectives.

How does the play work and what does it mean? That depends on whatever each collection of actors in each iteration of the course discovers that they want it to be.

Something similar occurred in my Dramaturgy course just this year. The previous year—the fall of 2016—the class, for obvious reasons, had chosen, as the theme for its hypothetical theatre company's five-play season, the dangers of incipient fascism. Not wanting to repeat myself, that option was not on this year's list. One option I gave them was the "Great Divide"—the socioeconomic gap between the one percent and the 99 percent. The students collectively persuaded me to let them combine that topic with the previous year's topic of fascism: that is, how does the socioeconomic divide, and society's neglect of the 99 percent, lead to a sense of disenfranchisement, which makes the population ripe to be seduced by an opportunistic proto-fascist demagogue?

As usual, individual play-readers and subcommittees reported on 15 to 20 Shakespeare plays which might fit the bill. One likely choice was *Julius Caesar*, which had become ubiquitous over the previous year and a half. I told them about Nicholas Hytner's 2012 National Theatre production of *Timon of Athens*, which reconfigured Alcibiades as the leader of a tent city of "Occupy" protesters. The most obvious choice, surely, was *Coriolanus*: the citizens revolt when the patricians hoard grain, the crowd is manipulated by its newly appointed tribunes, the patricians attempt to transform a military hero into a political leader, Coriolanus shows his contempt for the plebeians and ultimately leads an invasion of the city that had rejected and banished him.

But the students were not considering only those plays that tell the particular story they had chosen for their season, but plays *that could be made to* tell that story. They kept coming back to *King Lear*. It was neither the family drama nor the political infighting that struck them, but rather a single scene: Lear, now mad, first encountering the naked Poor Tom before the hovel. And they were struck by a single line: "O, I have ta'en / Too little care of this!" Lear's path to discovery through his madness might be one that leads him to the recognition of the social and economic injustices caused by his own neglect, inspiring him to want to "feel what wretches feel." Edgar might not be merely imitating an isolated bedlam beggar but joining a mass of displaced homeless people. The hovel could be a highway underpass or (like the wilderness outside Athens in Hytner's *Timon*) an abandoned half-finished construction site. The machinations of the royal family could be framed by a world populated by the dispossessed. Need the storm be a storm at all? It could just as easily be a crowd of people, a wall of humanity. Perhaps the crashes of thunder could be a passing express train barreling through an abandoned subway station.

I warned them that their approach to the play ran the danger of inverting the "figure-ground" relationship; that their bringing what was conceived as context into the foreground would leave a hole where the play's actual foreground action usually lives. They saw my point, but, admirably, stuck to their guns. The dramaturgical work they later did on the entire five-play season reinforced their decision. One play that they selected—Caridad Svich's dramatic adaptation of Isabel Allende's novel, *From the House of the Spirits*—reassured us that a multi-generational family saga could, by design, actually be telling a story about social and political change. Even more reassuring was the assignment to bring

in illustrative and inspirational photographs and images
that could be posted on the walls of the rehearsal room, and
which, later, could be used in lobby displays and programs.
For Lynn Nottage's *Sweat*, set in Reading, Pennsylvania,
before and after the local factory closes, several students
brought in photographs of declining American cities. One
particular image—the abandoned rowhouses and vacant lots
of Detroit, with the GM Renaissance Center glittering in the
distance—struck us as the perfect image for our *King Lear*.

Is the "story" that *King Lear* is "telling" a story about
the disenfranchisement of the 99 percent fueling a populism
that empowers tyranny? Certainly not. But that (or something like it) was a story the play *could* tell. Such a story
should not be measured by its fidelity to the story the script
was telling in its original context. The students' interpretation, as Hartley says, was self-authorizing. And their loyal-
ties as dramaturgs belonged not to the play as written but to
the story the production they were working on chose to tell
with the script.

Of all of the periods, histrionic languages, scenographic
conventions, and aesthetic schools the students study in
my Shakespeare Performance History seminar, the greatest
challenge, and (for me) the greatest fun, is having them
read William Henry Ireland's notorious Shakesperean forgery, *Vortigern*, which John Philip Kemble produced and
acted in at Drury Lane Theatre in 1796. By the time the
play was actually performed, Edmund Malone had already
exposed it as a fraud, and Kemble, now convinced that he
had wasted time, money, and talent on a forgery, famously
mocked the play while performing in its single disastrous
performance. But, for a while at least, Kemble, along with
many other readers, historians, antiquarians, scholars, and
theatre people including his sister Sarah Siddons (who had
been scheduled to act in it but dropped out of the project a
week before the opening), accepted what they were reading
as Shakespeare with enough confidence that the playwright
and theatre-owner Richard Brinsley Sheridan was willing to
pay a substantial sum for the exclusive performance rights,

and Kemble was willing to muster all the resources of his company to learn it, rehearse it, and mount it.

How could Kemble and Sheridan have mistaken such an awful play for Shakespeare? The answer lies in the fact that they were reading the script, not for its literary values, but for its theatrical craft—for situation, conflict, passion, pathos, character, psychology, picture, and spectacle. To better understand this, I have the students, before they read *Vortigern*, read Kemble's pamphlets comparing *Richard III* and *Macbeth*, descriptions of Siddons's Lady Macbeth (if only they were familiar with *King John*, I'd have them read descriptions of her Constance), and chapters of Joseph Donohue's still-useful *Dramatic Character in the English Romantic Age*; and I show them theatrical portraits, along with toy-theatre character sheets and tinsel prints, so that they can appreciate how actors build performances around "points." Only then can the students read *Vortigern* through the eyes of theatrical professionals in Britain at the end of the eighteenth century. Only then can the students understand why, for those theatre artists, in that time and place, *Vortigern* was Shakespeare as they wanted Shakespeare to be.

I consider myself lucky that fortune has freed me from having to teach a standard Shakespeare survey course.

Why bother asking questions about the art, craft, and "meaning" of the "original" play as the "original" "author" "intended" it? (I use scare quotes with the intent to scare.) Such questions are answerable, just as one can give a numerical answer to the question, "What is two plus two?" But I'd much rather teach my students to ask questions which they can answer with a question: "What did they—what do you—what do *I* want it to be?"

It's more theatrical that way. It's more empowering, And besides: it's just more fun.

### References

Barton, John. *Playing Shakespeare*. London: Methuen, 1984; DVD re-issued by Athena, 2009.

Dessen, Alan C. *Elizabethan Drama and the Viewer's Eye*. Chapel Hill: University of North Carolina Press, 1977.
———. *Recovering Shakespeare's Theatrical Vocabulary*. Cambridge University Press, 1995.
Donohue, Joseph W., Jr. *Dramatic Character in the English Romantic Age*. Princeton University Press, 1970.
Hartley, Andrew James. *The Shakespearean Dramaturg: A Theatrical and Practical Guide*. New York: Palgrave, 2005.
Mazer, Cary M. *Double Shakespeares: Emotional-Realist Acting and Contemporary Performance*. Madison, NJ: Fairleigh Dickinson University Press, 2015.
Miller, Jonathan. *Subsequent Performances*. New York: Viking, 1986.

# 15

# "Who's There?" "Nay, Answer Me. Stand and Unfold Yourself": Attending to Students in Diversified Settings

## Naomi Conn Liebler

I should begin with an explanation of my title. This essay will have nothing to do with *Hamlet*, from which the lines are borrowed; it is directed instead toward the reciprocities of teaching Shakespeare's work to diverse groups of readers—diverse in backgrounds, interests, educational backgrounds, and opportunities. I appropriate Shakespeare's lines here because they speak to a range of experiences and responses that themselves might be said to typify—if that is even possible—how some of my students have experienced their engagements with Shakespeare. The lines from *Hamlet* open the play, and are spoken by Bernardo and Francisco, two sentinels on watch—unsure for (or against) what—on the castle walls at Elsinore. They are of course old friends, but in the dark and the cold in the middle of the night, muffled against the elements, they do not immediately recognize each other. Francisco challenges his comrade to "stand and unfold" himself. In thinking about how I have been teaching Shakespeare's plays, and to whom, for nearly half a century, it occurs to me that "stand[ing] and unfold[ing]" themselves is what I have asked the plays to do, and it is also what

I have asked my students to do. The texts and the situations represented in Shakespeare's plays often seem at best strange and alien to their own language and experiences, if not completely cloaked and unrecognizable. My challenge as their teacher has been to facilitate their requirement that these texts reveal themselves to their uneasy readers. In confronting each other—often in the cold and in the dark, so to speak, wary of an unfamiliar challenger—Shakespeare's plays and my students often seem to dance around each other, a little guarded, a little nervous, hoping that it will all turn out OK and no one will die from it.

It goes without saying that teaching Shakespeare to students at secondary or undergraduate and MA levels is a remarkably varied experience, depending, of course, on the "composition" of the class. Our students bring themselves, their distractions, their personal problems, their experiences to their reading, their seeing and hearing, and so I have found the practice of engaging them in the *utile et dulce* of Shakespeare study to be an incredibly and unpredictably rich experience, regardless of the "level" of the class or its members. We read out of who we are.

My university began in 1908 as a Teacher Training Institution; 20 years later it became a State Teachers College; 30 years after that, a "liberal arts" college with a consistently strong teacher-preparation agenda and a small master's program; by 1994 it had become a State University, and in 2016 became both a Carnegie-classified "public research university" and a US Department of Education-designated "Hispanic-Serving Institution." Increasingly we are called upon to be, if not all things to all people, then at least as many things as we can manage to as many people as we can reach.

Two growth tendencies, first toward multicultural representation in curriculum and in population, and more recently toward a consciously architected diversity in student and faculty populations representing a variously defined "America," have brought about some curious reconsiderations regarding the practice of and the reasons for teaching Shakespeare's work. We are abetted by the curricular requirements of middle and secondary schools in the State of New Jersey that continue to insist upon the study of Shakespeare at those levels. As we train and certify a large percentage of the teaching populations in the state, accordingly we teach Shakespeare to some extent in order to prepare *our* students to teach Shakespeare to *their* (future) students. In many ways, it's been a very comfortable niche to occupy, and despite shrinking enrollments overall, courses in Shakespeare seem to remain "safe" from the scythe of deanly enrollment managers. In my department, we don't *require* our students, not even our English majors, to take a Shakespeare course, but the folks who certify K-12 teachers *do* require one course in Shakespeare, and despite a growing trend among our undergraduate English majors toward professions other than teaching, K-12 pedagogy remains a popular enough career plan to sustain our Shakespeare sections. We keep these classes small (a cap of 33) and tightly organized around discussion rather than lecture. We don't employ teaching assistants; the three Shakespeare instructors do their own teaching and their own marking. We serve around 100 students every semester at the undergraduate level. These statistics have remained constant over the 46 years I have been teaching here.

But everything else has changed, and continues to change: not *what* I teach, but *how* I teach it, and more importantly, *to whom*.

Increasingly, I find that I am not so much "delivering" Shakespeare to my heterogeneous and ethnically/racially diverse student populations as I am tapping into what they already know, experientially, in order to clear a path for them to forge their own connections. I want them to own what they read, to make it their own. They certainly can, and in a gratifying number of cases they do. The touchstone term used to be "relevance"; now it's "relatability." Whatever the word, the underlying demand is, for some reason, some justification for all the work involved in learning what is effectively a new language, certainly a new syntax and grammar, and whole new sets of backstories and metrics: what has this to do with *me*; why should I bother (or even care)? Cultural capital? This is not *my* culture and it's not *my* capital.

I have known from the very start of my teaching life that if I could not answer those questions with integrity and a good deal of respect for my students' skepticism, I should probably find some other way to pay my rent. I have not always succeeded in making the difference to my Shakespeare students that I wanted to make, and sometimes the jury stayed out for a decade or longer. I don't always *know* what difference I or Shakespeare have made to them. But I do know that those students have made a profound difference to me, enough to keep me in the classroom beyond the useful life of my paperback teaching editions inscribed with my excitedly scribbled and beloved marginalia and crumbling pages that long ago lost both front and back covers, prompting more than a few students to offer to take up a collection to buy me new copies. This essay, then, is not about the teaching methods or pedagogical practices that ease my students' way into expertise—or whatever it is that we formally hope for. It's about how the conversations among us—teacher and students—have merged and synthesized a collection of specific relationships within the shared experience of studying plays, so that Shakespeare comes to mean *something* to each of us. We are all reading the same plays, but we are all reading them differently.

I am thinking of two quite different teaching experiences that have made lasting impressions on me. One was with a group of local secondary and middle school kids brought to my campus for "Humanities in the Schools Day," a program of half-day "conferences" for secondary and middle school students and their teachers presented by Montclair State University's Institute for the Humanities, which ran some 70 sessions for 25 years between 1992 and 2017. These schools have some latitude in selecting the plays they will teach students between 8th and 12th grades, but the true constant appears to be *Romeo and Juliet*, and so, especially because the group in my charge on one December afternoon in 1999 was mainly 8th- and 10th-graders, that was the play of choice. It was not my intention to teach them "about" the play, nor to preempt the work of their own classroom teachers. I had no way of predicting or even learning what prior work they had done or what challenges or roadblocks they might have encountered. To some extent, this was going to be a one-size-fits-all conversation, and I hoped it would fit everyone in the room, some of whom were from homogeneously white suburban communities and others from inner-city urban schools. I should note here that when I delivered this workshop, school districts in my part of New Jersey had not yet banned *Romeo and Juliet* from their curricula and removed copies from their library shelves, as some have now done because of a concern that the play might seem to be promoting teen suicide, or teen sex, or teen elopements—or "teen" rebellion of any kind.[1] The subject of suicide or rebellion was not raised that day; my own agenda was not to rehash the discussion points already available in their own classrooms but rather to suggest another perspective, one that had informed my own thinking about Shakespeare for nearly a decade at that point, derived from my reading of Victor Turner's revolutionary explanations of liminality in *The Ritual Process: Structure and Anti-Structure* and others of his books. This remains an important core of what I talk about when I talk about Shakespearean tragedy, and I have introduced the concept at every level of classroom discussion from undergraduate through MA courses. That day, I introduced it to these middle and high school students. The idea that tragedy occurs when one is stuck in an incomplete passage from one status (social, political, biological, etc.) to another seemed simple enough and appropriate enough for these 8th- and 10th-graders, and they absolutely "got it." There was not an adolescent in the room who did not recognize the dangers of such a passage, or did not know that in fact that's what adolescence *is*: *liminality*, a time and a state of transition, when identities and expectations and even "rules" are ambiguous and confusing. Liminality renders the subject confused and confusing, endangered and dangerous. They are not what they were, and not yet what they will be. While in transition, as all teenagers are, they need such protections as their cultures and communities can provide for them. This is never about blame or fault. It is never the responsibility of any individual. Because it encompasses passages and transitions on which the survival of a community depends, seeing the principals through that transition, via rituals and practices designed by culture to protect that vulnerability, is the responsibility of the whole community: it does indeed take a village. When structures of authority can't or don't perform their responsibilities, tragedy happens. In *Romeo and Juliet*, it's not the kids' fault. This was in sum the focus announced in a flyer distributed in advance to the teachers:

> The tragedy of *Romeo and Juliet* is above all the tragedy of Verona; at the end of the play, the two young lovers are united forever in death, but the community represented in the Montague and Capulet families has lost its next generation. As the prince says at the play's end, "All are punished." Are the two kids merely "poor sacrifices" to a community's internal war, or are they in some ways partly responsible for what happened to them and their bereaved families? The failure of the entire city to honor and protect its own rituals, designed to protect and ensure the continuation of the community, is the core of this tragedy.

Some of the teachers were visibly unsure about this idea—they had not come across it before—but it was absolutely clear to me that the kids understood exactly what I was talking about. One 8th-grader within earshot stage-whispered: "She *way cool!*" The play unfolded for them. They recognized the crucial issues laid out in text and performance. Ours was a "class" with an unconventional and for the most part unanticipated structure, but teaching and learning got done that day.

The second circumstance involved a young graduate student named Marcos Vargas who came to us to find the answers to a question put to him as he introduced his own inner-city secondary classes to *Othello*. Mr. Vargas was teaching English in a high school in Newark (the state's largest and most diverse urban center). When one of his students, unfamiliar with the term "Moor," asked him whether Othello was a black man, Mr. Vargas said he didn't know but would find out. That promise brought him to my university and to my graduate class on Shakespearean tragedy. (Because we did not allow auditors in our graduate classes, he had to enroll in the MA program in order to take the course!) He went on to write a thesis under my direction on negotiations of race in Shakespearean drama titled *Mending the Moor on the Early Modern Stage: The Rise of Shakespeare's Black Tragic Hero* (2007). Even while the thesis was in progress, Vargas brought his lessons to the Newark and Irvington (NJ) schools of which he was himself a graduate:

> I was the fresh grad student. I had already been a teacher by trade for several years ... While I never struggled with getting the words out in an academic setting, in fact I relished the opportunity, [studying Shakespeare] made it clear to me that precision and substance must always accompany verbosity. As the realization that this would be no easy "A" began to take hold, so did my fiery resistance to mediocrity ... For myself, I expected more and resisted settling for less. For my students, I demanded their best and by doing so demonstrated my respect for them ... I no longer lead classrooms; I lead school districts now.[2]

Marcos Vargas became chair of the English department in the Newark public school where he taught, then District Supervisor for English Language Arts 6–12 for Irvington, a community next to Newark that has been classified by the State Department of Education in the lowest of eight levels of socioeconomic opportunities for education. He is now the Director of Secondary Education for the Montclair, New Jersey, Public Schools, where he oversees curricula encompassing English Literature, English Language Arts, and English as a Second Language. For Vargas, the lessons learned from studying Shakespeare, from engaging closely not only with the language but, perhaps more import- antly, with the perpetually knotty and urgent questions of living vibrantly in a threatening world, have created a legacy of continuing educational influence that he passes on to his students, to the teachers under his supervision, to their students, and so on. The lessons retained and passed along are the things that matter now—not plots of plays or character analyses, and probably not speeches memorized (though that can still happen by choice and resonance). Heroic models, inspirations toward persistence and resistance and to deliberative thought and reflection are what my students, and Marcos Vargas's students, find engaging and meaningful.

There have been and doubtless will continue to be other examples of how a life informed by reading, hearing, seeing, and thinking about Shakespeare shows a number of high-water marks over time. I'm sure that everyone contributing to or reading this volume has them. For me, there was one more (so far) very recent event that will remain a high point in my Shakespearean career. The extraordinarily gifted director Karin Coonrod brought to our campus last fall (September 2017) her radical and unforgettable production of *The Merchant of/in Venice*, and the university made a two-week celebration of it, capped by an evening of conversation among two colleagues—David Kastan of Yale and James Shapiro of Columbia—and Supreme Court Justice Ruth Bader Ginsburg. I had the pleasure of introducing their conversation by explaining to a select audience of donors, local luminaries, politicians, a State Supreme Court Justice, and a few members of the general public why this production mattered—why Shakespeare mattered. These were not, in the main, our students; they were members of a public whose taxes support what we do, and who had every right to wonder what they were paying for. Here is the last part of what I said, in trust that it will also serve to conclude this essay:

> *The Merchant of Venice* is a play that looks closely at issues of inclusion, diversity, and the consequences to a community that scapegoats and bullies and would homogenize those it *allows* to live in it. It's obviously a play for our time, and it is very much a play for our

campus, for our students, and for our surrounding communities (plural). In my teaching, I ask my students to find *something* in the plays they are studying, the characters and situations represented, that they can recognize in themselves. I want them to own what they read, to find their own way in, to see that, apart from a few linguistic distractions, a few "thees," "thous," and "those," Hamlet or Othello or Shylock or Antonio "R" us. They really R. No one ever asks me (though I know the question is out there somewhere) why we still study Shakespeare, and why we study Shakespeare at Montclair State. Here's my answer anyway. It's because he knows us, knows who we are now. We don't just talk about Shakespeare as a dead carver of cultural relics, though there's some of that too. He also helps us to understand ourselves. Now. It's not like we've changed all that much.

## Notes

1 A quick Google search reveals the (often anecdotal) urban-mythic scope of reports of this phenomenon, perhaps best known from Sara Munson Deats' path-breaking essay, "The Conspiracy of Silence in Shakespeare's 'Romeo and Juliet,'" in *Youth Suicide Prevention: Lessons from Literature*, eds. Sara Munson Deats and Lagretta Tallent Lenker (New York: Plenum Press, 1989).
2 Marcos Vargas, personal communication, November 2016.

# 16

# Unpicking the Turkish Tapestry: Teaching Shakespeare in Anatolia

## *Patrick Hart*

We must not think the Turk is so unskillful,
To leave that latest, which concerns him first.
                                    (*Othello*, 1.3.28–29)

People claim Turks are macho, but Lady Macbeth
Scares patriotic, patriarchal Turks to death.
It belongs to Turks: this scepter'd isle of John Bull,
Stratford on Avon is as dear to us as İstanbul,
We're involved: Lear can blame us, Richard can maim us;
Iago can defame us, the shrew can tame us.
Shakespeare, like Atatürk, condemned those who make spears:
They both sang loving praises of those who break spears.
Our nation is Atatürk's but also Shakespeare's.
                                    (Talât S. Halman)[1]

### "Shakespeare de yasak"—Shakespeare forbidden too

As I sat down to write this paper in the run-up to the parliamentary and presidential elections of June 2018, a Shakespeare news story was hitting some of the few remaining Turkish press outlets still publishing stories critical of Erdoğan's government. Deniz Yılmaz had been detained without trial since the spring for protesting Turkey's offensive against the Kurdish enclave of Afrin in northern Syria (the operation codenamed, in a paradigmatic case of Orwellian newspeak, "Operation Olive Branch"). Deniz was doing his best to continue his studies in his prison cell, in the hope he might be released in time to sit his end-of-semester exams at Istanbul's Boğaziçi University. When his family brought his copies of Shakespeare's poems and plays to the prison, however, the guards confiscated them, and refused to release them back to him.[2]

Studying Shakespeare is not as difficult for the majority of our students as it has been for Deniz. The obstacles the state places in their way are less dramatic. English Language education is poor: in the EF English Proficiency Index for 2018, Turkey is ranked 26th out of 27 European nations, above only Azerbaijan, with "very low" proficiency (the lowest category), and 62nd out of 80 ranked countries overall.[3] My students' mastery of English varies widely, from near-native competency to little more than elementary. For many, parsing Shakespeare's language presents significant challenges. The Turkish school system privileges rote learning over thoughtfulness, originality, and the construction of nuanced arguments. Evaluation takes the form of multiple-choice exams demanding the identification of a single correct answer, discouraging the development of anything akin to negative capability. Most high school students graduate with little or no experience of writing argumentative, literary essays in Turkish, let alone in English. Most schools also offer little exposure to drama. None of this is ideal preparation for the study of Shakespeare, though it does generate a helpful hunger for play.

With the ongoing state of emergency impinging ever more upon the lives of my students, however, and our little academe ever more under threat,[4] the political situation and the cultural politics behind it overshadow all else, and keeping politics out of the classroom feels neither possible nor desirable. The question is in what form to admit it. Presentism is a perpetual temptation. The questions that Stephen Greenblatt's *Tyrant: Shakespeare on Politics* (2018) sees the plays as repeatedly posing echo my students' laments. Why does "evidence of mendacity, crudeness or cruelty serve not as a fatal disadvantage but as an allure, attracting ardent followers? Why do otherwise proud and self-respecting people submit to the sheer effrontery of the tyrant, [...] his spectacular indecency?"[5] As Greenblatt demonstrates, Shakespeare time and again depicts the terrible price of these submissions: the putrefaction of public and private morals, the killings, the devastating economic expense. Many students cannot resist identifying Macbeth or Caesar with Erdoğan, and Scotland or Rome with modern Turkey. More than one student has drawn parallels between Erdoğan's desire for extended presidential powers (successfully realized through the constitutional referendum of April 2017) and Caesar's supposed intention to transform Rome back into a monarchy.

But to read—or worse, to teach—Shakespeare's tyrants as proxies for Erdoğan can be as calamitous as to read them as proxies for Trump. Particularities and differences get elided, and existing prejudices are confirmed and projected onto and into the text. There are of course subtler, less palatable political lessons the plays can teach any opposition, when those particularities and differences are brought into focus. As Rhodri Lewis (who nails the dangers of Greenblatt's approach) observes, Brutus and his companions "convince themselves that they are acting from principle [...] yet they are also fighting to preserve their privilege and status." Ultimately they fail because they "fall victim to the delusions of self-righteousness and moral vanity," a lesson many feel segments of the opposition in Turkey would do well to learn.[6]

Discussions ostensibly about Shakespeare can quickly slide into what are transparently debates over contemporary Turkish politics and culture. Usually I try to give these debates room, partly on the grounds that there is so little safe space for them elsewhere. But no space here is entirely free, and in addition to guarding against the spilling over of classroom tensions, I need to ensure as tactfully as possible that students don't say anything that might conceivably get them into trouble if reported outside the classroom. The avoidance of specifics in such discussions can be as amusing as Greenblatt's refusal to actually name Trump in *Tyranny*, though far darker. Usually students circle back to the play eventually, though not always with the panache of one who, quoting Cicero, suggested that the kind of appropriation her fellows were making, "constru[ing] things after their fashion, / Clean from the purpose of the things themselves" was itself a symptom of "strange-disposèd" times—whether Rome in 44 BCE, London in the final years of Elizabeth's reign, or Ankara today. The importance of staying alert to such misconstruals, she suggested, was the real lesson the play could teach us.

If a self-aware presentism can lead to such insights, it is the deeper influence of Turkey's polarized cultural politics on how both my students and I approach Shakespeare that has come to strike me as the fundamental, inescapable issue with which my own pedagogical practice must engage. I work in a department shaped by Talât Halman, Turkey's first ever Minister for Culture (1971), who also served for many years as Chair of English Literature here at Bilkent. Arguably Turkey's leading translator of Shakespeare, he was an unabashed bardolator of great learning and kindness, and made Shakespeare the keystone of the curriculum. Halman was also an avowed supporter of the legacy of Ataturk: he celebrated the founder of the modern Turkish state as a "secularist visionary," a "humanist," and "the hero of a 20th century-renaissance." Inspired by Ataturk, the "Turkish nation," he concluded, "will not allow the religious fundamentalists, fanatics, and zealots to create an oppressive regime."[7]

Personified in Talât Halman's career, the alignment of Ataturk and his legacy with humanism, with the Renaissance, and above all with Shakespeare still carries immense weight here, all the more so because it is rarely explicitly articulated. Turkey offers an intriguing (if not straightforward) example of how for "non-western" cultures the notion of renaissance serves not merely as a metaphor for cultural rebirth, but comes to represent "a transformation that must eventually culminate in a modern, national, and, in some degree, westernized (or globalized) culture."[8] That in such scenarios the Renaissance tends to be disproportionately *English* tallies with the extent to which processes of modernization have been inseparable from the global spread of English. Established to counter the Ottoman political and religious order, Kemalist Turkish nationalism, founded on supposed links between Turks, the Turkish language, and the soil of Anatolia, found an analogue in English nationalism's appropriation of Shakespeare as the national poet of England's green and pleasant land.

The very persistence of the "Shakespeare" course (we have no other compulsory course dedicated to the work of a single writer) implicitly supports this view of Shakespeare as prophet and paradigm of western modernity, as does my role as the privileged English instructor. And it is this model of a rationalist, secular, enlightened Shakespeare that still prevails here, at least in the elite universities and the schools in the wealthier urban centres from which Bilkent draws many—though by no means all—of its students. Yet under Erdoğan's rule—all my students have ever known—there has been a deliberate, programmatic reorientation towards distinctively Ottoman and specifically Muslim cultural practices and art forms, and a corresponding downplaying of the value of western cultural models and inspirations. Of course, not only is the tapestry of Turkish cultural attitudes of a far more complex weave than this sketch allows for; it is precisely the crude reduction of these complexities (which this overview threatens to replicate) by the dominant discursive regime to a series of Kemalist/neo-Ottomanist dichotomies that does as much to exacerbate Turkey's "culture wars" as it does to describe them.[9]

I am still struggling with the pedagogical implications of all this. Shakespeare's privileged position in the canon and the curriculum raises issues everywhere, but here these issues take on a particular hue. Unsurprisingly, the sense of Shakespeare's significance that my students bring to class is often immensely conflicted, even contradictory, and can play out in unpredictable ways. Cultural cringe struggles with national pride. Unexamined, this maelstrom of assumptions hampers engagement with the particularities of a given work. To begin to unpick these assumptions also means unpicking the students' sense of what both Shakespeare and I might represent, for them. I want to encourage students to question what I think of as the Halman model, and its implicit belittling of the Ottoman inheritance. But students angry or despairing about the political situation cling to it, and are understandably suspicious of any attempt to rehabilitate Ottoman culture, given how this has been weaponized for political ends. Yet there is also often suspicion too of this all-pervasive paradigm of western cultural authority.

If addressing the ideological and teleological elements to the teaching of Shakespeare presents challenges, though, failing to do so also means missing a pedagogical trick. Getting students to articulate and examine the assumptions they bring to their studies, where they might come from, and the contested position Shakespeare occupies within Turkey as well as in the Anglophone world, begins the process of weaving Shakespeare into the fabric of their lives. Familiar and alien, Shakespeare becomes a way for them to think through their own historical situatedness and, perhaps, to move beyond the dichotomies that dog Turkish cultural politics, to a reassessment of their attitudes to their own cultural history.

So I begin by asking my students to think about *why* they are studying Shakespeare, and in order to push past the initial, bland answers (usually because "he's the best" or "we have to") I get them to list as many different reasons, from personal motivations to the wider cultural and geo-political pressures and attractions working upon them. This usually brings up ideas and questions that then run as undercurrents throughout the course. For example, several students with great glee called my attention to memes mocking claims made by Kadir Mısıroğlu, an Ottoman Monarchist, that his research had revealed Shakespeare was a Muslim, "Şeyh Pir" (or "Sheikh Pir," meaning master or old man). For many students, these claims evidently demonstrated the absurdity of those who would re-orient

Turkey towards a mythical version of its Ottoman past, but who so lacked confidence in their argument that they had to attempt to appropriate Shakespeare to it. But they also gave me the chance to ask students about what was happening in Turkey in the late sixteenth century, and why one might feel the need to claim Shakespeare, and why no one really talks of an Ottoman renaissance.

Sharing Walter Andrews' essay on the "Suppressed Renaissance" of the Ottoman sixteenth century (which I initially did as an afterthought) also proved surprisingly helpful in reframing our discussions. Subtitled "Q: When Is a Renaissance Not a Renaissance? A: When It Is the Ottoman Renaissance!", Andrews' study discusses why both Kemalists and religious conservatives have resisted describing the burgeoning of Ottoman culture from 1453 to 1625 as a "renaissance," even while recognising the term as a heuristic tool "seriously flawed by its inherent ideological complications."[10] The essay deals with material which students consider their own while offering new ways of critiquing both the neglect and the dismissal of the Ottoman legacy and its more recent politicized appropriations, ways that allow students to escape the Kemalist/neo-Ottomanist dichotomies.[11] While not ostensibly about Shakespeare at all, it helpfully models how students might historicize Shakespeare's cultural significance and recognize and think about debates around it. Revealing an American scholar's profound engagement with Ottoman culture and what it means for Turkey today, as well as my own hopefully open-minded interest in (and ignorance of) Shakespeare's Turkish contemporaries, and my willingness to learn what my students might have to teach me about them, also helps students regard our study of Shakespeare less as a culturally laden, even neo-colonial, imposition and more as a mutually supportive exploration.

Another example: in these discussions Buse, one of my most splendidly pugnacious and politically engaged students, told me straight out that she disliked Shakespeare because of his patriarchal attitudes, and went on to imply that his misogyny exercised a tyrannical influence over the whole culture and canon. My ongoing attempts to persuade her that Shakespeare's gender politics might be read another way, and her intelligent, good-natured resistance to these attempts, formed a helpful strand to class discussions of *Love's Labour's Lost* around which other students could structure their readings, coming in on one side or the other, or attempting to mediate between us. (Today, I'd point Buse towards Andy Kesson's argument for a more careful, even suspicious analysis of Shakespeare's place in contemporary theatre: his claim that it is "no accident that this playwright and his bizarre only-a-couple-of-women-per-play-thanks-very-much policy are at the heart of classical theatre" would strike a chord.[12])

The second way in which I have tried to encourage students to think about Shakespeare as always situated, contested, and available for appropriation is through an emphasis on creative processes of adaptation, transcreation, translation, and remixing. This applies to Shakespeare's own creative practices (his adaptations of Plutarch, Holinshed, and travel narratives, for example) and to the uses to which Shakespeare has been put on the stage, in film, in fiction, in painting, and elsewhere. This has also been in part a response to a chafing against the pervasive injunction to teach the text through performance. Practical experience has largely persuaded me of the arguments put forward by scholars such as Holger Syme, Andrew Hartley, and William Worthen, that performance and text are "simply incommensurable—that to conceive of a performance as an interpretation or realization of a text is a profoundly limited and theoretically problematic approach."[13] Thinking of performance in terms of adaptation, transcreation, and intermediality seems to offer a less problematic alternative. Most of all, though, getting students to participate for themselves in these processes of adapting, rewriting, and remixing encourages them to interrogate the various, often conflicting, assumptions they bring to Shakespeare and, paradoxically perhaps, to pay closer attention to the particularities of Shakespeare's own texts. It also lets them discover writing as "not the abstract cause or governing logos of the stage, but another kind of raw material—like lumber and canvas, or the theatre space, or even the actors' bodies—that is refashioned and resignified in the rigorously pragmatic working-out of the creative business of the playing."[14]

This has resulted in some intriguing remixes, such as the recasting of the final scene of *Hamlet* in the style of an episode from one of the TV shows set at the Ottoman court and wildly popular across the Middle East, or *Shakespeare's Measure for Measure: or, The Vindication of the Rights of Characters*, a rewriting informed by Mary Wollstonecraft and Luigi Pirandello, in which the allegiances of Shakespeare, who himself sits on the stage, are swayed over the course of the scene from the male characters to Isabella, who demands he rewrite her fate. One project in particular, though, pointed me towards one of the most effective methods I've yet found of helping EFL students to engage with the plays with confidence, and it's with this that I'd like to conclude.

When two bright students, İmge and Naz, produced a silent film adaptation of act 3 scene 1 of *Measure for Measure*, my curiosity was initially tinged with disappointment. One of my hopes in conceiving of the assignment had been to get students speaking Shakespeare's lines aloud, and these two Portias, it seemed, had found a loophole to get out of this, turning the letter of my instructions against me. Watching their film, though, and then discussing their project with them, showed me that they had understood the spirit of the assignment, perhaps better than I had myself. Influenced by Carl Theodor Dreyer's 1928 silent film, *La Passion de Jeanne d'Arc*, they had emulated cinematographer Rudolph Maté's use of unbalanced framings, white space, and dramatic angles to suggest unbalanced power relations and extremes of emotion. In doing so they activated suggestive correspondences between Isabella and Renée Jeanne Falconetti's Jeanne d'Arc, both figures assailed from all sides by patriarchal authority. By evoking *La Passion*, centred as it is upon Jeanne's trial, their scene also foreshadowed the final act of *Measure for Measure*, in which Isabella finds herself under arrest and under attack by the male representatives of the law and of state power, Angelo and the Duke.

The project, and İmge and Naz's commentaries upon it, revealed a sophisticated appreciation of Shakespeare's text, which also brought it to bear sharply on questions of gender politics in Turkey. But it also suggested how silent film specifically could serve as an excellent medium for helping EFL students engage with Shakespeare's plays. Much of the pedagogical value of this exercise comes from how it isolates individual processes of engagement and response. Selecting intertitles (those pieces of filmed, printed text edited into the flow of moving images) presents students with a practical exercise in critical reading and radical editing. From a scene of several hundred lines, they must identify no more than a handful to intersperse among their images. These need both to drive the action forward, filling in the gaps, and to work with and complement the visual images. That İmge and Naz managed to find intertitles that did all this while also retaining some of the most complex poetry of the scene demonstrated their skills as close readers and their instinctive understanding of the requirements and possibilities of the silent film's coupling of image and text. But the exercise had also suggested to them something about the playscript itself, about how closely bound together are word and action. This can be an exercise of great benefit to students experiencing more basic struggles with the text, too. Another, complementary option is for students to write concise summaries of the main action as prefatory intertitles, in the style of the 1909 silent adaptation of *A Midsummer Night's Dream*.

Having practical implications, the group discussions on intertitling prompts are usually focused and animated, and move organically from simple parsing of sense to nuanced considerations of how particular words, phrases, or speeches relate to the play's developing themes and concerns. Where multiple groups adapt the same scene, contrasting intertitling choices provide a concrete jumping-off point for discussions that return to the text.

Filming on mobile phones (several apps exist designed specifically for making silent films) put my students visibly at ease, and restored a sense of play. The possibility of multiple takes ameliorated performance anxiety, especially for those students less confident in their mastery of spoken English: several asked anxiously, "Do we have to use our first try?" and were visibly enthused on learning that they didn't. Freeing the students from actually speaking the lines also allowed them to concentrate on their bodily performances, on blocking, gesture, and facial expression. The demands and anti-realist conventions of silent film, in which gesture and expression are frequently exaggerated for communicative effect, in part to compensate for the absence of speech, gave the students additional licence, and helped them to overcome their inhibitions—particularly prevalent in a shame culture such as Turkey's.

There's much more to be said of such projects and the practical part they can play in the development of particular skills, but their greatest value, for me, lies in how they encourage students to claim the plays for themselves, without resorting to problematic notions of a universal or global Shakespeare. With the state of emergency now transformed into Agamben's perpetual state of exception under the new presidential system, I fear the obstacles my students will have to overcome to study Shakespeare will become ever greater, and perhaps even ever more dangerous. As they do so, the interrogation of the culturally embedded critical assumptions they bring with them, and of those of their teachers, will become ever more important. Looking back over this paper, though, I realize how much of it is not so much about how I teach Shakespeare as how my students have taught me to teach Shakespeare. I look forward to continuing to learn from them.

## Notes

1 Talât S. Halman, "Shakespearean Art in the Turkish Heart: The Bard in the Ottoman Empire and the Turkish Republic," in *Shakespeare 450*, ed. A. Deniz Bozer (Hacettepe University, 2014), 11–28: 16.

2 "Shakespeare de yasak," *BirGun*, June 4, 2018 <www.birgun. net/haber-detay/shakespeare-de-yasak-218308.html> (accessed

June 28, 2018); "Shakespeare'e cezaevi yasağı" (Shakespeare banned in prison), *Cumhuriyet*, June 3, 2018 <www.cumhuriyet.com.tr/amp/haber/turkiye/988517/Shakespeare_e_cezaevi_yasagi.html> (accessed June 28, 2018).

3  "English Proficiency Index," *Education First* <www.ef.com.tr/epi/> (accessed June 22, 2018).

4  "Turkey: Government Targeting Academics Dismissals, Prosecutions Create Campus Climate of Fear," *Human Rights Watch*, May 14, 2018 <www.hrw.org/news/2018/05/14/turkey-government-targeting-academics>

5  Stephen Greenblatt, *Tyrant: Shakespeare on Politics* (New York: Norton, 2018), 1–2.

6  Rhodri Lewis, "Fashion It Thus: Stephen Greenblatt's 'Tyrant,'" *Los Angeles Review of Books*, June 24, 2018 < https://lareviewofbooks.org/article/fashion-it-thus-stephen-greenblatts-tyrant/#!>

7  Talât S. Halman, "Ataturk as Immortal Hero," *The Turkish Times*, December 1, 1995, Year: 7, No: 150 <www.columbia.edu/~sss31/Turkiye/ata/halman.html> (accessed June 28, 2018).

8  Walter G. Andrews, "Suppressed Renaissance," in *Other Renaissances: A New Approach to World Literature*, eds. Brenda Deen Schildgen, Gang Zhou, and Sander L. Gilman (Basingstoke: Palgrave Macmillan, 2006), 29–30.

9  My terminology here is again borrowed from Walter G. Andrews, "Stepping Aside: Ottoman Literature in Modern Turkey," *Journal of Turkish Literature* 1 (2004), 9–32, 9–10.

10 Walter G. Andrews, "Suppressed Renaissance," in *Other Renaissances: A New Approach to World Literature*, eds. Brenda Deen Schildgen, Gang Zhou, and Sander L. Gilman (Basingstoke: Palgrave Macmillan, 2006), 29–30.

11 My terminology here is again borrowed from Walter G. Andrews, "Stepping Aside: Ottoman Literature in Modern Turkey," *Journal of Turkish Literature* 1 (2004), 9–32, 9–10.

12 Andy Kesson, "Galatea, BritGrad and diverse alarums," *Before Shakespeare*, June 4, 2018 <https://beforeshakespeare.com/2018/06/04/galatea-britgrad-and-diverse-alarums/>

13 Holger Syme, "Using Performance to Teach Shakespeare," *dispositio*, January 10, 2016. <www.dispositio.net/archives/2257> (accessed June 22, 2018).

14 William B. Worthen, *Print and the Poetics of Modern Drama* (Cambridge University Press, 2006), 3.

# 17

# Teaching Shakespeare to Retirees in the OLLI Program

## *Alan C. Dessen*

My first experience on the teacher's side of the room was in September 1959 as a spanking new graduate student teaching Freshman Composition, a task for which I had no rhetorical or pedagogical preparation. Each class was a major effort so that the result was a series of exhausting but exciting challenges. My final contact with undergraduates was in April 2005 in classes on *The Tempest* and *'Tis Pity She's a Whore*. After 45 years I would not describe myself as burned out, but a lot of the fun and anticipation in walking into the classroom had disappeared, and, though the students may not have noticed, I was recycling material rather than reengaging with it. Two years later, an experiment in teaching a short course on three Shakespeare plays to retirees in a program at Duke University convinced me that I was not ready to get back into the saddle.

The situation had changed in 2010 when I returned to that same program at Duke, now part of the national OLLI program (Osher Lifelong Learning Institute), and, as of March 2018, I have finished my fifteenth course (once-a-week 90-minute sessions for 10 weeks) and, to my surprise, have managed to squeeze in 35 of the 37 canonical plays (*Timon of Athens* and *Henry VIII* have been left out in the cold). In that process I have discovered that teaching retirees and senior citizens has its ups and downs—and thereby hangs my tale.

I already had some experience teaching adults in roughly 20 years of informal courses at the Oregon Shakespeare Festival (sometimes with an actor as co-teacher). In one format in the 1980s (entitled "Wake Up With Shakespeare") our group saw a series of productions and discussed them the following morning. Little preparation was required (I just started by throwing a piece of raw meat onto the table), and the major problem was keeping the discussion within bounds. Teaching Shakespeare's plays at OLLI was a much bigger challenge and demanded considerable preparation and different strategies.

In Oregon, and especially at OLLI, the big difference from my years in the university classroom was teaching Shakespeare's plays to people with life experience. I have taught *The Tempest* twice over these eight years and both times have had the best experience in my career with that magical play. Miranda's line "O brave new world / That hath such people in it" is justly famous, but we have had some intense discussions of Prospero's easily ignored response: "'Tis new to thee" (5.1.183–184).[1] Two of my regulars are retired lawyers who on occasion provide expert commentary. One of them explained how he had used Portia's undoing of Shylock in the trial scene in a workshop for would-be trial lawyers. He also clarified a distinction important in act 2 of *Henry VI*, Part 1, between a nobleman being *attached* or being *attainted* for treason against the king. I got some expert testimony from a retired pathologist on the possibility of poisoning through the ear in *Hamlet* (he was dubious, though here I could argue that symbolism-imagery trumps real-world practice).

The tastes, skills, expectations, and backgrounds of the "students" vary widely. Some participants in my early OLLI years could not handle email, but more recently I have found that many have IT skills much superior to mine. I have had complaints from some who prefer reading plays as poems in dramatic form and therefore want more time spent on close analysis of the text (and a fellow OLLI instructor has had great success devoting the entire term to one Shakespeare play). That approach is how I was taught as an undergraduate in the 1950s in the age of what was then termed New Criticism, but my regulars (a dozen or more) enjoy my performance-oriented approach. A few already have a solid grounding in the plays and the period, whereas others are beginners getting their first close look at a Shakespeare play.

Here I am reminded of an anecdote from Stratford-upon-Avon when, after 15 minutes, an American gentleman walked out of a performance. The staff in the foyer, all atwitter, asked what was wrong; he replied: "Nothing. I just wanted to see a little Shakespeare." For me, finding a Goldilocks zone for targeting my clientele—not too hard, not too easy—has been impossible, so that teaching the three parts of *Henry VI* to a smaller-than-usual group posed a major challenge (and I was pleased that my least-informed regular ended up enjoying the trio as history).

The major bane for those who have toiled for years in departments of English is reading and then putting grades on the work of students—and I am no exception. Indeed, my complaints had become a standing joke to some of my colleagues. The greatest appeal of my time in the OLLI program has been the absence of papers and examinations and also the absence of committees and administrative duties—and, I confess, after many years *committee* had become a four-letter word. The result is all the joy of being in the classroom without the hassle.

Another major plus is that no one is *required* to take my OLLI course. Rather, people sign up and pay for the opportunity (currently $90 for ten sessions), so that the clientele choose to be there and pay for the privilege, as opposed to undergraduates grudgingly confronting unfamiliar names, blank verse, and early modern usages. As a result, the major problem in teaching undergraduates (establishing the value of your course to those merely trying to fulfill a requirement or an empty slot) is eliminated. As had been true in the not-for-credit Oregon summer courses, having participants who choose to be there and have paid for the privilege can make a huge difference to the atmosphere and the give-and-take in the classroom.

The down side of both the absence of grades and the sign-up process is reflected in attendance. Experienced participants in this OLLI program often enroll in multiple courses as a shopping maneuver, then drop out, usually without giving notice to the teacher. Meanwhile, with no final exam or final grade, those who lose interest along the way have no imperative to finish the course or read plays carefully. Rather, the most popular offerings that draw large audiences consist of lectures on history ("World History of the 1930s"), current events ("The World Today"), or practical matters ("Illness, Aging, and Death"), titles drawn from the winter 2018 catalogue.

In addition, not all the "students" have retired, so that conflicts with their working lives can emerge, and medical appointments can take precedence, as can illness and family issues. People in this age group regularly go on vacations that can last for weeks. A very enthusiastic enrollee recently apologized for missing the final classes on *Twelfth Night* because 1) one morning he had a business appointment in another city and 2) on another his first grandchild had just arrived (not the kind of response one expects from an undergraduate). My mantra has been that we are not engaged in a degree program: "This is OLLI." Walking into a session that has 25 students officially enrolled I never know how many faces will be confronting me when I start my spiel.

Other problems include weather-related class cancellations during the winter term (in 2015 I lost two class sessions from a ten-week course) and malfunctioning equipment for showing scenes via DVD or streaming. However, my clientele is forgiving and, even if I sometimes press the wrong button on the remote control, we muddle through.

In my first decade of teaching after graduate school I was regularly assigned large lecture courses with as many as 400 students, a format I grew to dislike. Indeed, I still remember vividly the moment during some introductory comments on *Hamlet* when I said that there were four reasons for the many controversies and, after citing number three, wandered off with an anecdote. When I came back to "Reason number four is ..." roughly 350 students who had been sitting back to take in the anecdote in unison bent over and put pen to paper in preparation for what they thought might be on the next exam. That moment scared me. I had given the signal and they had responded, but that response belied what I thought *Hamlet* and teaching was all about.

Whenever possible I therefore avoid lecturing or talking too much. Nonetheless, I put a lot more work into these sessions than is necessary in that I send long, detailed emails (two or three pages single-spaced) in advance of each class with background material and comments, along with questions drawn from my reading and playgoing that do not have easy answers—and feedback from my clientele tells me that these messages are welcomed. Not every question is answered or even addressed in the subsequent class, but I can hope that seeds have been planted. For example, in a recent email I devoted a sentence to the question: should Sir Andrew Aguecheek exit after Sir Toby's dismissive comments in 5.1 or stay onstage? Short on time (see below), we did not discuss that question, but normally I would have used the pause button to stop when, in the wintry Kenneth Branagh version, Andrew with a bloodied face watched the union of Olivia and Sebastian.

Taking a performance-oriented approach in the class-room brings with it an assortment of problems, especially for someone like me who has no talent as an actor or director (as opposed to my colleagues elsewhere who are adept at handling such in-class action). My method (and I hesitate to use that term for what I am doing) has evolved since the late 1970s, when the BBC TV series became available to our library on those unwieldy and unreliable three-quarter-inch cassettes. Here there be dragons, for from the start until now, each class has been vulnerable to equipment failure. I have another vivid memory of two strong undergraduates gladly carrying the bulky TV monitor and cassette player down two flights of stairs when the elevator was out of commission because they much preferred watching and discussing a few scenes than hearing me natter on for 45 minutes. In my OLLI classroom I have had almost every conceivable glitch with equipment, recalcitrant DVDs, or finding the right spot to begin on a DVD or streaming show. Many of the early BBC versions have chapter breaks only at the end of each act, so that in 2010 my attempt to begin with *Measure for Measure* 2.4 meant that (with no fast forward or rewind function available) I had to play through all of act 2 at normal speed before class to get to my desired starting point.

The other major problem in building on scenes worthy of discussion is finding suitable DVDs or online versions. Working with often-produced plays such as *Twelfth Night*, *Hamlet*, and *Macbeth* is no problem, but now that equipment in my classroom has switched exclusively to playing DVDs, my collection of VHS tapes is less of an asset. However, with the help of a colleague I am exploring the alternative of downloading VHS scenes to a flash drive to be played on my laptop. New shows do keep turning up, but for some items the BBC series is still the only workable option (and on Netflix even lesser-known plays often have "long wait" attached). The problem is even more severe if I try to include one or more plays by Shakespeare's contemporaries. Again, a few well-known items are available (*Volpone*, *The Duchess of Malfi*, *The Changeling*), but when I included Kyd's *The Spanish Tragedy* in a course on Revenge plays all I could find was one scene on YouTube.

In spite of such difficulties, I have stuck with my scenes-in-class model because when it works there can be a big pay-off—and access to the pause button to get feedback is a huge pedagogical plus. Recently I included *The Merry Wives of Windsor*, a play that I had never taught before but had often enjoyed on stage. The text is mostly prose, rather than blank verse, but the language and frame of reference of suburban Windsor provide a major challenge for a first-time reader. As anticipated, I had some grumbling, even from my regulars, and some parts of the BBC production do not come off well, but key scenes involving the two wives (played adeptly by Judy Davis and Prunella Scales) and Ben Kingsley's Ford set up my thesis about comedy and entertainment—and seeing how the women outsmarted the men proved to be a big hit for my group, a feature that had much less impact in their reading.

When searching for an available version for class use, the original BBC 37-play collection is sometimes the only choice (for example, for *Troilus and Cressida*). Some of the weakest renditions are of major plays (*Romeo and Juliet, As You Like It, Antony and Cleopatra, Othello, The Winter's Tale, The Tempest*), but for them there are often other choices available. However, various less-traveled roads can be gems (*All's Well That Ends Well, Pericles, Cymbeline*, the three parts of *Henry VI*). To focus on scenes that have the potential to generate discussion can turn a less than overwhelming production into a useful pedagogical tool. I have taught *Two Gentlemen of Verona* twice as an archetypal early comedy and in the process found the BBC Julia (Tessa Peake-Jones) the best I have ever seen, a big hit in my class. The BBC *King John* works well as a history play or in a problem play context.

The spate of movies initiated by Kenneth Branagh's *Henry V* has added to the pool of possibilities, but here, too, problems can arise. I understand the need for adjustments when moving from the original playscript to cinema, but even though I do not push my own scholarly agendas, my theatre historian gene is never fully recessive. The Ralph Fiennes movie of *Coriolanus* has many virtues, but the movie does not do justice to the final scene, a moment that continues to fascinate me, so that the fuller text in the BBC version can be a major asset. Similarly, both of the more recent BBC *Hollow Crown* ventures provide some remarkable actions and interactions (as played by Jeremy Irons and Tom Hiddleston, the face-off between Henry IV and Prince Hal in *1 Henry IV*, 3.2, is the best rendition I have ever seen), but the first movie in the second trilogy that covers both Part One and Part Two of *Henry VI* runs just over two hours, whereas the running time of Jane Howell's two equivalent BBC shows is six and a half hours. Lost in that process are many of my pet scenes in the two plays (and the BBC Part One, 2.3, the Countess of Auvergne scene with Talbot, is another gem).

To bring a performance awareness into the classroom often leads to changes. For years I had sidestepped teaching

*Macbeth* because I thought that I had little to add to what students already knew from high school, but in the early 1980s a colleague supplied me with a taped-off-the-air copy of the Thames TV version of the theatre production directed by Trevor Nunn and starring Ian McKellen and Judi Dench. I had seen this show at the Young Vic in 1978 at the end of its run and still think it the best rendition of a Shakespeare play in my 50 years of playgoing. The TV version does not catch all of that in-the-theatre experience, but several moments are indelibly etched in my memory—particularly McKellen's rendition of "being gone, / I am a man again" in the banquet scene and Dench's "O, O, O" as part of her sleepwalking (3.4.106–107, 5.1.52). Sharing those moments with students of all ages became a significant part of my teaching.

A recent experience with teaching comedy also comes to mind. In looking for new combinations of plays (some of my regulars have been with me for most of my offerings) I decided to include four comedies that I had rarely if ever taught and climax with three weeks on *Twelfth Night*. I did get access to the BBC versions of the earlier items, so that we had fun with *The Comedy of Errors, Two Gentlemen of Verona*, and *Merry Wives*, though *Love's Labours Lost* (despite much effort on my part) was not a success (and I realized why I had never before dealt with it in the classroom). My original plan was to devote the third session on *Twelfth Night* to the last scene and end the course with the final 15 minutes of the 1993 Trevor Nunn movie. I already had a DVD that had been put together for a special presentation that had excerpts from three shows, and I also streamed a segment from the 2014 London Globe. In the past I had success including two or three versions of the same scene or segment (especially for the prayer scene in *Hamlet*), but never before had I tried to squeeze in five.

Repeating more or less the same lines to gain very different effects proved to be rewarding and enjoyable. The upbeat BBC show ends in sunlight and song; the version directed by Kenneth Branagh ends with a remarkable Malvolio (Richard Briers) ragged, halting, and squinting at the light and Anton Lesser's Feste departing in a snowstorm;

in an older show Alec Guinness's Malvolio vows revenge, but at his exit he earns a laugh when he pulls up one of his yellow stockings to the accompaniment of tinkly music. What was particularly instructive for me and my students was the varying treatment of Olivia's "Most wonderful!" (5.1.225). In the Branagh and Guinness versions, the two words are perfunctory. In Tim Carroll's 2014 all-male London Globe show, Mark Rylance got a huge laugh as he collapsed onto a bench to cap off a very funny sequence. In the Nunn movie that I had saved for last, the reaction to the appearance of Sebastian and the reunion with Viola (a moment handled as well as I have ever seen it done) was enhanced by the camera panning over the faces of Orsino, Antonio, and Ben Kingsley's Feste, but the high point was Helena Bonham Carter's wide-eyed, show-stopping delivery of "Most wonderful!" In my emails I regularly point out that early modern writers thought of *admiratio*-wonder-amazement as the essence of comedy and romance, but no glosses were necessary to feel the wonder here—a truly magical moment.

In March 2018 I chose to finish my course on a climax with *Coriolanus*, another play that can pose difficulties for first-time readers but which fit well with the focus that term on the warrior–hero. Here the availability of three DVD versions (with two of them available to watch at home) made a huge difference and generated a series of lively discussions about the body politic then and now. After the last class a student who had been relatively quiet during our sessions spoke to me about his experience. He had a strong science background, but confessed that as a reader he had been bored with Shakespeare in both high school and college and could not understand what all the shouting had been about. Watching scenes in the classroom and full productions at home (particularly the Dench–McKellen *Macbeth*) had been a revelation, and in spite of the difficulty of language and syntax, he had been fully engaged by *Coriolanus*. He was eager for more, a response welcome to any teacher.

In conclusion, some of the OLLI clientele have had a lot of experience with these plays, but others struggle, especially with the history plays (and *Love's Labour's Lost*). However, putting pivotal scenes on screen can level the playing field and often elicits reactions that surprise me and make me rethink what I thought I knew. Passions can run high. In a recent class, one of my favorite students, a contrarian who always had her own take on issues, took offense at another whose remark she deemed sexist, and threw her glasses case across the room (he caught it deftly)—an electric moment that I really enjoyed. Being in a room with people who care a lot about these plays is a high point of my teaching career.

I have no idea how long this final phase will last. My voice is sometimes unreliable; my hearing is no longer what it should be; my memory is not to be trusted; and at the end of the day after a 90-minute class I sometimes feel brain-dead. Still, if the in-class adrenalin keeps kicking in, I hope to continue. In Touchstone's words: "much virtue in *if*."

## Note

1 Citations from Shakespeare are from *The Riverside Shakespeare*, ed. G. Blakemore Evans, 2nd edition (Boston and New York: Houghton Mifflin, 1997).

# Afterword: "Cur Non?"

## June Schlueter

In the preceding pages, 20 scholars and theatre practitioners spoke of how and why they teach Shakespeare. Their essays bristle with ideas that offer a vision of the text as both literary object and performance script. Editor Sidney Homan joins twenty-first-century faculty who see Shakespeare's plays as central to the practices of reading and seeing and who recognize that there are as many ways to interpret Shakespeare as there are readers. Cary Mazer, who, with the rest of us, once routinely asked, "What is the meaning of this scene or phrase?" now casually but consequentially asks, "What do you want it to be?" As Andrew Hartley points out, students need to understand that a play, by its nature, is "fundamentally plural." In place of the thesis-driven approach to meaning, Hartley and his students explore what the text might become. Along with the literary "Why?", they ask the theatrical "Why not?"

Sidney Homan's *How and Why We Teach Shakespeare* is an invitation to each of us to see Shakespeare as a collaborator with everyone intent on extracting meaning from his plays. In the introduction to this collection, Homan reprises each of the essays, noting that among today's teachers of college- and university-level Shakespeare, questions are every bit as important as answers. Whether thinking of the text as a script for actors, revealing special ways of examining the script, exploring Shakespeare through performance, or adjusting one's approach for different classrooms, all 16 contributors agree that the performance possibilities provided by a Shakespeare play offer multiple paths to understanding. All agree that the playwright who has for generations been a staple—now *the* staple—of the English curriculum richly deserves our attention.

But how did Shakespeare find his way into the college curriculum in the first place? Interestingly, I spent my career at the college that has the answer. In the decade preceding the start of the Civil War, Francis A. March (1825–1911), reputedly the first person in this country to hold the title Professor of English, began teaching Shakespeare. He was a member of the Faculty at Lafayette College in Easton, Pennsylvania, named in 1826 for the Marquis de Lafayette, the friend of the American Revolution whose personal motto was "Cur Non?"—"Why not?"

March had a question too: "Why not teach English like the Latin and Greek?" To modern ears, the question sounds almost disingenuous, but at the time it was a revolutionary concept, for English—language and literature—had little authority in the classroom. March accomplished so sweeping a change that the weekly journal *The Independent* averred that opportunities to study English at Lafayette were "the best in the country"; the *British Quarterly* noted that "nowhere else" was the subject treated with "equal competence and success"; and the *London Athenaeum* praised March's instructional methods, which "are not surpassed by those which we are accustomed to associate with the German universities."[1] March, who was on the Faculty at Lafayette for 51 years, retiring in 1906, declined repeated invitations to move to major universities, though he accepted honorary degrees from Princeton (1870 and 1896), Columbia (1887), Cambridge (1896), Oxford (1896), and others, including Amherst College, his alma mater (1871).

At Lafayette and elsewhere, March's colleagues were teaching the Classics, in Latin and Greek, which, March remarked, "were thought to be the proper languages to study."[2] March was fluent in these and other languages, but his specialty was Anglo-Saxon, that is, Old English or early medieval English, and he was interested in bringing the mother of our mother tongue into the classroom. His landmark book, *A Comparative Grammar of the Anglo-Saxon Language* (1870),[3] suggests the kind of work he was attempting: it was nothing less than a profoundly detailed comparative analysis of the English language with other major Indo-European tongues. As Kemp Malone noted, March "laid the foundation on which all future historical grammarians ... were destined to build, and his fame will ever rest secure as ... the founder of a science."[4]

March's interest in teaching Anglo-Saxon complemented his interest in teaching English literature, particularly works by Chaucer, Shakespeare, and Milton. As Gerald Graff points out, the task of Classics professors in the mid-nineteenth century was to instruct "gentlemen of good breeding" who, when exposed to passages of great poetry, would know intuitively what the work's belletristic meanings were: there was no need to offer instruction in interpreting "hidden meanings."[5] But March had other ideas. Why, he asked, can't Shakespeare's plays be studied "after the same methods as Homer and Demosthenes?"[6]

In 1865, March published "Method of Philological Study of English in Lafayette College," in which he explained that philological study entailed "careful scrutiny of every word"; students "regularly look up the etymology of every word, and prepare for questions on its history and its relations to kindred words in other languages, the phonetic laws which govern the changes of form, the laws of thought which govern the changes of meaning, historical inferences to be drawn from it, and similar matters."[7] A year earlier, in *Method of Philological Study of the English Language*, he presented his analysis of act 1 scene 1 of *Julius Caesar*, apparently the first Shakespeare play to appear on his syllabus.[8] The questions he asked of his students covered a range of biographical, psychological, cultural, historical, and literary questions, such as these:

Where was [Shakespeare] born? What kind of place is Stratford geographically—*e.g.*, is it by any river, by the sea, by mountains, flat, hilly, sandy, marshy, barren, fertile, quiet, stormy, the horizon near or remote, capable of what sunrises, sunsets, storm-scenes, and the

like? What kind of place was it botanically—*e.g.*, how
wooded, cultivated, how as to wild plants, flowers? What
residences there or hard by—*e.g.*, town-houses, country-
seats, castles? What literary opportunities—*e.g.*, libraries,
schools teaching what? Why are these questions asked?
Have they any thing to do with the development of
Shakespeare's genius? How so? ...

> When was *Julius Caesar* written? Was it probably
> a long time growing in the mind of Shakespeare?
> What lesson is it intended to teach? What conspiracies
> in England during the life of Shakespeare? On the
> Continent? What friends of Shakespeare connected with
> any of them? What in his relations to Elizabeth and
> James would add interest to the matter? Was it a subject
> to please the people? Is there evidence in other plays that
> the story of Caesar had long made a deep impression on
> his mind? ... Could not a good drama be written closing
> with the assassination of Caesar? Could it teach the
> same lesson as this play?[9]

After two and a half pages of similar "background" questions,
he moves to a (painfully) close linguistic analysis of the
opening lines, beginning:

> What is the first clause? What ellipsis? ... What kind
> of clause—declarative, interrogative, imperative,
> exclamatory, or optative? ... What is the verb? ... Subject?
> ... What does hence combine with? Kind of combination?
> ... Does it complete or extend the predicate? ... Is it an
> adjunct of time, place, mode, or cause? ... What language
> is it from? ... What is the root letter? ... Why called a
> pronominal element? ... What other words in English of
> the same pronominal element—pronouns? ... Adverbs?
> ... Of what case does –ce represent the ending? ... What
> other adverbs ending in –e? ... How was this genitive
> ending written in Anglo-Saxon?[10]

These questions continue for 28 pages (!) before March
moves to the opening lines of scene 2.

March is thought to have been the first in the country to include a Shakespeare play on his syllabus. His description of his approach to meaning in Shakespeare is detailed in *The Dial* essay:

> In a play of Shakespeare, for example,—and one term is regularly devoted to a play of Shakespeare,—a scene, a short scene, may be given out for a morning's study. A considerable part of it will be read rapidly, or the gist of it given in a few words, and most of the hour will be devoted to a few lines selected as worthy of thorough study. Any obsolete words or phrases, or singular constructions, will be explained; but the secret of Shakespeare's power is not to be found in these. The words which are bearers of special meaning or feeling are usually familiar words. In searching for their power and charm, the student will trace them through all the places where Shakespeare uses them, using the Concordance to bring them all together. He will use the Historical dictionary to learn what associations had gathered around them in the earlier ages, beginning sometimes in *Beowulf*, and accumulating as they pass to Alfred, to Chaucer, to Tyndale, to Spenser ... He will often find that the peculiar meaning in Shakespeare begins with him, and then it will be pleasant to trace it in later authors, repeated in quotation or allusion until it becomes perhaps the most familiar meaning.

In the end, students would be led "livelily to rethink the thought and perceive and feel and remember the beauty of the language."[11]

High-minded, to be sure, but utterly impractical. What twenty-first-century student, accustomed to the instantaneous results of online searches, would take an hour to study a few lines, a morning to study a scene, a semester to study a play? What student would ask (much less answer) the hundreds of questions March asked of *Julius Caesar*? I am sure this is not what Nick Hutchison had in mind when he encouraged his students to "play the specific, not the general" and urged "close textual questioning."

Indeed, philology today has become a historical curiosity. Nonetheless, 40 years ago, when I was a doctoral student at Columbia, I had a personal taste of March's pedagogy. The syllabus for my Shakespeare course with S. F. Johnson listed 16 plays for which students would be responsible. But at the end of the semester, we were still on the first act of *Romeo and Juliet*, the first play on the syllabus. At the time, though I admired the range of the professor's knowledge, I found his parsing of every element of a word or phrase pedantic. For years afterwards, I told the story of Prof. Johnson's syllabus, always to an amused audience. It was only after my husband and I edited a collection of March's essays[12] that I realized Prof. Johnson was participating in the academic tradition that March began.

Francis March's method of teaching Shakespeare may no longer be viable, but it is hard not to admire the mastery of detail and the breadth of knowledge the discipline of philology demanded. Nor can we dismiss the field's insistence on inquiry. Indeed, the impulse to question not only remains current in today's classroom; it has become dominant, as the contributors to *How and Why We Teach Shakespeare* repeatedly reveal. Whatever the impact of philology on teaching today, twenty-first-century Shakespeareans can be grateful to Francis March for having opened his classroom door to Shakespeare and for asking "Cur Non?"

## Notes

1 Quotations are in David Bishop Skillman, *The Biography of a College: Being the History of the First Century of the Life of Lafayette College* (Easton, PA: Lafayette College, 1932), 1:232–233.

2 Francis A. March, "The Study of Anglo-Saxon," in *Report of the Commissioner of Higher Education* (Washington, DC: US Bureau of Education, 1876), 475–479.

3 Francis A. March, *A Comparative Grammar of the Anglo-Saxon Language, in Which its Forms Are Illustrated, by those of the Sanskrit, Greek, Latin, Gothic, Old Saxon, Old Friesic, Old Norse, and Old High German* (New York: Harper & Brothers, 1870).

4 Kemp Malone, "March, Francis Andrew (Oct. 25, 1825 – Sept. 9, 1911)," in *Dictionary of American Biography*, ed. Dumas Malone (New York: Scribner, 1923–1936), 12:268–270.

5 Gerald Graff, *Beyond the Culture Wars: How Teaching the Conflicts Can Revitalize American Education* (New York: Norton, 1992), 128–129.

6 Francis A. March, "English at Lafayette College," *The Dial*, May 16, 1894, 294–296.

7 Francis A. March, "Method of Philological Study of English in Lafayette College," *American Journal of Education* 16 (September 1866): 559–568.

8 Francis A. March, *Method of Philological Study of the English Language* (New York: Harper & Brothers, 1865), 37–65.

9 March, 37–39.

10 March, 39–65.

11 Francis A. March, "English at Lafayette College."

12 Paul Schlueter and June Schlueter, eds., *Francis A. March: Selected Writings of the First Professor of English* (Easton, PA: Friends of Skillman Library, Lafayette College, 2005). Several passages in this Afterword were previously published in this volume.

# About the Contributors

**James C. Bulman** is Professor of English at Allegheny College. General editor of Manchester's *Shakespeare in Performance Series*, he has written a performance history of *The Merchant of Venice* (1991) and edited anthologies on *Shakespeare on Television* (1988), *Shakespeare, Theory, and Performance* (1996), and *Shakespeare Re-Dressed* (2007). His most recent publication is *The Oxford Handbook of Shakespeare and Performance* (2017).

**Joseph Candido** is Professor of English at the University of Arkansas. He has published extensively on Shakespeare and Renaissance drama. He is the editor of the *King John* volume in the Bloomsbury Press series *Shakespeare: The Critical Tradition* (1996), and recently he has edited *The Text, the Play, and the Globe: Essays on Literary Influence in Shakespeare's World and His Work in Honor of Charles R. Forker* (Fairleigh Dickinson/Rowman & Littlefield, 2016).

**S. P. Cerasano** is the Edgar W. B. Fairchild Professor of Literature at Colgate University and the editor of the annual volume *Medieval and Renaissance Drama in England*. She has written extensively on theatre history in England, 1580–1630, and particularly on playhouses, playhouse owners, and theatrical culture. Most recently, she completed the Norton Critical Edition of Shakespeare's *Julius Caesar*. She is also the co-editor, with Steven W. May, of *In the Prayse of Writing: Early Modern Manuscript Studies*.

**Alan Dessen** is the Peter G. Phialas Professor Emeritus of English at the University of North Carolina, Chapel Hill. He is the author of eight books, four of them with Cambridge University Press: *Elizabethan Stage Conventions and Modern Interpreters* (1984); *Recovering Shakespeare's Theatrical Vocabulary* (1995); *Rescripting Shakespeare* (2002); and, with Leslie Thomson, *A Dictionary of Stage Directions in English Drama, 1580–1642* (1999). He has been the editor or co-editor of the "Shakespeare Performed" section of *Shakespeare Quarterly*.

**Jerry Harp** is Associate Professor of English at Lewis and Clark College. His books include *For Us, What Music? The Life and Poetry of Donald Justice* (2010) and *Constant Motion: Ongian Hermeneutics and the Shifting Ground of Early Modern Understanding* (2010). He has published four books of poetry, the most recent of which is *Spirit under Construction* (2017).

**Patrick Hart** is co-founder and editor of the *Journal of the Northern Renaissance*, and an Assistant Professor of English Language and Literature at Bilkent University in Ankara, Turkey. He is currently working on European film adaptations of early modern literary texts, and has also translated Elsa Morante's long poem, *La canzone degli F.P. e degli I.M. in tre parti*, as "The Song of the Happy Few and of the Unhappy Many, in three parts" (Transference, 2008). At Bilkent he has participated in a number of dramatic productions involving both faculty and students.

**Andrew James Hartley** is the Robinson Professor of Shakespeare at the University of North Carolina, Charlotte. He is the author of *The Shakespearean Dramaturg* (Palgrave), *Shakespeare and Political Theatre in Practice* (Palgrave), and a performance history of *Julius Caesar* (Manchester University Press). He is the editor of *Shakespeare on the University Stage* (Cambridge University Press), *Shakespeare and Millennial Fiction* (Cambridge University Press), and the Arden *Julius Caesar: A Critical Reader*. He was resident dramaturg for Georgia Shakespeare, and is a popular novelist.

**Sidney Homan** is Professor of English at the University of Florida and his university's Teacher/Scholar of the Year. The author of eleven books and editor of five collections of essays on Shakespeare and the modern playwrights, he is also an actor and director in professional and university theatres. His most recent book is *Comedy Acting for Theatre: The Art and Craft of Performing in Comedies*, with the New York director Brian Rhinehart (Bloomsbury/Methuen).

**Nick Hutchison** is a freelance director, actor, and lecturer on Shakespeare. His professional directing credits include shows at the Sam Wanamaker Theatre, the Folger Theatre in Washington DC, and the American Shakespeare Center in Virginia, among many others. He is an Associate Tutor at the Royal Academy of Dramatic Arts, and co-director of their eight-week Shakespeare course, and is Course Director for the Royal Conservatoire of Scotland and for the University of Notre Dame at the Globe.

**Russell Jackson** is Emeritus Professor of Drama at the University of Birmingham. His books include *The Cambridge Companion to Shakespeare on Film* (Cambridge University Press, 2007), *Shakespeare Films in the Making: Vision, Production and Reception* (Cambridge University Press, 2007), *Theatres on Film: How the Cinema Imagines the Stage* (Manchester University Press, 2013), and *Shakespeare and the English-Speaking Cinema* (Oxford University Press, 2016). His research is informed by his extensive experience in professional theatre and film as text consultant for productions by a number of directors, including Kenneth Branagh and Michael Grandage.

**Frederick Kiefer** is the University Distinguished Professor at the University of Arizona in Tucson. His published work includes *Fortune and Elizabethan Tragedy* (1983), *Writing on the Renaissance Stage* (1996), *Shakespeare's Visual Theatre: Staging the*

*Personified Characters* (2003), *Masculinities and Femininities* (2009), and *English Drama from Everyman to 1660: Performance and Print* (2015).

**Kristin Kundert** is Associate Professor in the University of Georgia's Department of Theatre and Film Studies. Professionally, she has worked as a producer, director, vocal coach, and actor. Her work in Shakespeare companies includes: The North Carolina Shakespeare Festival, The Virginia Shakespeare Festival, and The Kingsman Shakespeare Festival in Los Angeles. She co-authored *Action! Acting Lessons for CG Animators*.

**Naomi Conn Liebler** is the University Distinguished Scholar and Professor of English at Montclair State University, where she specializes in Shakespeare, Early Modern English Drama, World Drama, and Literary Theory. She is the author of *Shakespeare's Festive Tragedy: The Ritual Foundations of Genre* (Routledge, 1995), editor of *Early Modern Prose Fiction: The Politics of Reading* (Routledge, 2007) and *The Female Tragic Hero in Renaissance English Drama* (Palgrave, 2002), and co-editor of *Tragedy: A Critical Reader* (with J. Drakakis, Longmans, 1998).

**Cary M. Mazer** is Professor of Theatre Arts and English at the University of Pennsylvania. He has directed the plays of Euripides, Shakespeare, Webster, Strindberg, Shaw, Barrie, Pinter, and Beckett. He is the author of *Shakespeare Refashioned: Elizabethan Plays on Edwardian Stages* (1981), *Double Shakespeares: Emotional Realist Acting and Contemporary Performance* (2015), and *Great Shakespeareans XV: Poel, Granville Barker, Guthrie, Wanamaker* (2013). His play, *Shylock's Beard*, won the 2016 Association of Theatre in Higher Education Award for Excellence in Playwriting.

**Paul Menzer** is a professor and the director of the Mary Baldwin University MLitt/MFA Shakespeare and Performance graduate program. He is the editor of *Inside Shakespeare: Essays on the Blackfriars Stage* (2006), author of *The Hamlets: Cues, Qs, and Remembered Texts* (2008), *Anecdotal Shakespeare: A*

*New Performance History* (2015), and *Shakespeare in the Theatre: The American Shakespeare Center*. His plays *Anonymous, The Brats of Clarence,* and *Shakespeare on Ice* have appeared on the Blackfriars stage and his *Invisible Inc.* at the Long Center for the Performing Arts in Austin, Texas.

**June Schlueter** is the Charles A. Dana Professor Emerita of English at Lafayette College. Her most recent book, with Dennis McCarthy, is *"A Brief Discourse of Rebellion and Rebels" by George North: A Newly Uncovered Manuscript Source for Shakespeare's Plays*. With James P. Lusardi, she published *Reading Shakespeare in Performance: "King Lear"* and edited the *Shakespeare Bulletin* for 20 years.

**Liam E. Semler** is Professor of Early Modern Literature at the University of Sydney and leader of the Better Strangers/Shakespeare Reloaded project, which is a collaboration between the school Barker College in Sydney and academics based at the University of Sydney, the Australian National University, and James Cook University. He is author of *Teaching Shakespeare and Marlowe: Learning versus the System* (Bloomsbury, 2013) and various essays on early modern literary studies and education.

**Fran Teague** is Meigs Professor and University Professor at the University of Georgia. Her principal area of research is Shakespearean performance history and theory. Teague often serves as a dramaturg for productions by the university, as well as local theatre companies. Her books include *Shakespeare's Speaking Properties* and *Shakespeare and the American Popular Stage*, and her articles have appeared in *Theatre Survey*, *Shakespeare Quarterly*, and *Shakespeare Studies*.

**Erica Terpening** is a director, actor, and writer. She is the Co-Artistic Director of the Shakespeare company Anon It Moves Theatre in Portland, Oregon; literary manager for Portland Actors Ensemble; co-founder of Singing House Productions in Lafayette, Colorado; and the former Managing Director of the off-Broadway company The Strain Theatre in New York. Last year, she produced and directed "_____," *an Opera*, an experimental new work with an improvised musical score for Singing House Productions.

**Miranda Fay Thomas** is Assistant Professor in Theatre and Performance at Trinity College Dublin. Her first monograph, *Shakespeare's Body Language: Shaming Gestures and Gender Politics on the Renaissance Stage*, will be published in 2019 by Arden. She has also contributed chapters and articles to *The Palgrave Handbook of Shakespeare's Queens* and *Early Modern Literary Studies*. Since receiving her PhD in 2016, she has taught at St Anne's College, Oxford; the University of Greenwich; Central School of Speech and Drama; King's College London; University College Dublin; and Shakespeare's Globe.

**Beth Watkins** is Professor of Theatre at Allegheny College. She has directed over 60 plays, including several by Shakespeare, and published essays in such places as *Theatre Journal*, *Theatre Topics*, the *Journal of Medical Humanities*, and *Performing Adaptations*. In 2013, her *Playing Dirty* won awards for Outstanding Production of a Devised Work and for Distinguished Performance and Production Ensemble at the Kennedy Center American College Theater Festival.

# Index